PRACTICAL ORGANIC GARDENING

Practical **ORGANIC** Gardening

MARK HIGHLAND

COOL
SPRINGS
PRESS

Brimming with creative inspiration, how-to projects, and useful information to enrich your everyday life, Quarto Knows is a favorite destination for those pursuing their interests and passions. Visit our site and dig deeper with our books into your area of interest: Quarto Creates, Quarto Cooks, Quarto Homes, Quarto Lives, Quarto Drives, Quarto Explores, Quarto Gifts, or Quarto Kids.

Inspiring | Educating | Creating | Entertaining

© 2017 Quarto Publishing Group USA Inc.
Text © 2017 Mark Highland

First published in 2017 by Cool Springs Press, an imprint of The Quarto Group, 401 Second Avenue North, Suite 310, Minneapolis, MN 55401 USA. T (612) 344-8100 F (612) 344-8692 www.QuartoKnows.com

Cool Springs Press titles are also available at discount for retail, wholesale, promotional, and bulk purchase. For details, contact the Special Sales Manager by email at specialsales@quarto.com or by mail at The Quarto Group, Attn: Special Sales Manager, 401 Second Avenue North, Suite 310, Minneapolis, MN 55401 USA.

10 9 8 7 6 5 4 3 2 1

ISBN: 978-1-59186-687-9

Library of Congress Cataloging-in-Publication Data

Names: Highland, Mark, 1977—author.
Title: Practical organic gardening / Mark Highland.
Description: Minneapolis, MN : Cool Springs Press, 2017. | Includes bibliographical references and index.
Identifiers: LCCN 2017029502 | ISBN 9781591866879 (hc)
Subjects: LCSH: Organic gardening.
Classification: LCC SB453.5 .H537 2017 | DDC 635.9/87—dc23
LC record available at https://lccn.loc.gov/2017029502

Acquiring Editor: Mark Johanson
Editor: Bryan Trandem
Content Editor: Katie Elzer-Peters
Project Manager: Alyssa Bluhm
Photo Assistance: Barb Pederson
Art Director: Brad Springer
Cover Designer: Mark Reis, Percolator Graphic Design
Page Design and Layout: Laura Shaw Design

Printed in China

Contents

01

Benefits of Organic Gardening—It's Not Just about Food

Civilizations have gardened for millennia. Ever since the first domestication of plants—the point where people realized they could plant seeds and tend them into productive growth rather than just forage randomly—people have been farming in some fashion to support their own sustenance.

It was farming that allowed civilization to develop initially because it allowed tribal units to remain in the same place rather than moving about constantly, as was true in the hunter/gatherer stage of human history.

Without food, we have no chance of existence on the planet, and without farmers we have no food. This primal, basic need for food gives us a stronger primal connection to agriculture and gardening than to any other industry or pastime.

◁ Grow your entire garden and landscape organically.
Don't just limit organic methods to the vegetable garden.

In the early centuries of farming/gardening, all practices were "organic" in that providing nutrients for plants and controlling diseases and pests were done with naturally occurring substances. Insect pests were either killed by hand or perhaps by encouraging natural predators. Early farmers learned that rotating crops kept soil from wearing out, and that fertilizing with decaying organic (formerly living, carbon-based) material would rejuvenate soil and cause plants to grow better.

It was not until farming became a commercial enterprise and technology developed to a point where specialized chemicals could be refined that farming and gardening entered the non-organic stage. Highly artificial pesticides and fertilizers came into widespread use in the mid-nineteenth century, when John Bennet Lawes, a British entrepreneur, patented the first artificial "manure" by treating phosphates with sulfuric acid in 1842. As society's skill with refining chemicals increased over the next 100 years, so did the use of synthetic chemicals to jolt plants into greater growth and kill insect pests in prodigious numbers.

In the years just prior, during, and after World War II, synthetic pesticides came into widespread use to join synthetic fertilizers. Initially, the world believed it had found a non-toxic solution to pest control that increased yields by killing insects. Soon, though, we would begin to recognize this as hopeful but misguided. Pesticides began to accumulate in animal tissues and research would soon show that these chemicals had devastating effects on humans and wildlife. But this recognition would take several decades to become well known.

By a measure of sheer volume, the quantities of synthetic chemicals used on agricultural crop fields worldwide has steadily increased since the mid-1800s, and continues to increase to the present day, with usage exploding exponentially over the last 50 years, largely because previously underdeveloped areas of the world are now adopting more modern farming techniques. So it is clearly a hopeful error to imagine that organic farming practices are now somehow beginning to reverse the trend toward synthetic chemical use.

Yet as far back as the early 1900s, when the use of synthetic chemicals was just gaining steam, there were people recognizing the harmful effects of their use and attempting to counteract their effects. A movement called *biodynamic agriculture* came into vogue in 1924 in response to farmers who were noticing the ill effects of chemical use on their crops and livestock—and on the health of their families.

This movement toward natural farming has never waned and in fact has evolved into today's organic farming/gardening movement—in direct proportion to the increasing use of synthetic chemicals on a large scale.

Today, the interest in organic farming and gardening techniques is at an all-time high and growing. Most supermarkets have robust sections of their stores devoted to organically grown produce, and for home gardeners, growing their own organic produce has become the most popular and rapidly growing segment of the gardening market.

It should be noted that this book will focus on organic horticulture as it applies to the home gardener. Organic gardening is not the same as organic farming,

which takes place on a much larger scale. While they share many of the same tenets, organic gardening and organic farming are not the same. This book focuses on practical organic gardening, so the advice and techniques described herein are for the backyard organic gardener.

△ Organic gardening improves the health of the broader ecosystem surrounding your home and landscape.

The Renaissance of Organic Gardening

The modern era of organic consciousness perhaps began with the publication of *Silent Spring*, the book that deserves the most credit for documenting the changes occurring in agriculture and nature during this post–World War II era. As the name of the book implies, the author, Rachel Carson, wrote about the disintegration and eventual loss of nature's usual symphony orchestrated in springtime. From birds to frogs to insects, the natural world had grown considerably quieter after just over a decade of rampant pesticide use. Bird populations declined, insect populations declined, and the average backyard took on an eerie silence.

Back then, companies were promoting pesticides as the perfect solution to make people's lives better. This is a time when children innocently played in clouds of DDT vapor as city crews drove through the streets in tanker trucks spraying clouds of pesticides to control disease-causing mosquitoes.

In many cases, they were correct in saying human life was made better through discoveries in chemistry. There are many applications for chemistry that do not involve organic gardening that have improved quality of life for humans on this planet. The widespread use of plastic building materials has reduced devastation

△ Native plants are important components of organic gardens, helping to tie the tended landscape to its surrounding natural ecosystem.

of forests, for example. Of course, there are also examples of how chemistry has decreased quality of life for us in our daily lives—pollutants off-gassing from materials in our homes and offices, spewing out of our transportation system, and residing in the conventional food we eat. Even organic farms rely on chemistry in more than a few ways—diesel for fuel, plastic covering for greenhouses, plastic-based covers for protecting crops from winter's cold, and other chemistry-based technologies that help organic gardeners and farmers produce food.

Chemistry itself is not the enemy, but chemicals that degrade soil, water, and air quality should all be examined closely—as we finally realized in the late 1960s when we saw that bald eagles were disappearing from our landscape; that no longer were the warm summer evenings filled with the flicker of fireflies and the chirping of tree frogs; that some once-plentiful songbirds had become rare sights; that local farmers and others were being stricken with unusual cancers and other diseases.

Society's reaction to these very real problems caused by synthetic chemicals are at this very moment helping to reverse some of these trends. The Great Lakes and many rivers are now cleaner than they were 30 years ago, and the fish in them may be eaten safely. In many regions, bald eagles are once again a familiar sight. Regulations now seek to prevent wholesale pollution of the landscape, and some insidious forms of cancer are now on the wane.

It is into this portion of the epic social story that today's organic gardener fits—a gardener devoted to minimizing his or her impact on the environment at large, and seeking to improve the health of the family by consuming wholesome produce grown at home. Even if you're just a family of one. And there have never been more members in this socially conscious group than there are today.

The Principles of Modern Organic Gardening

Sustainability is the primary philosophy of organic gardening, based on the interconnectivity of gardening and gardens to the surrounding environment. Its roots are the phrase *Primum non nocere*, which in Latin means, "First, do no harm." This phrase reverberates throughout the organic gardening community because individual organic practices should build on each other to create an overall garden system that only increases in productivity over time. Productivity means crop yield, but it also can be quantified by other increases. For example, another positive outcome would be an increase in songbird visits to your garden when you grow organically, resulting from the greater quantity of edible insect life available for birds to feed on.

Organic gardens benefit local environmental conditions and build soil health over time, amassing soil carbon levels, building soil structure, and building soil microbial populations. This interconnected network of microbes converts organic substances to plant-available nutrients, and holds these nutrients in the soil until they are needed by plants.

Joining the practice of organic gardening involves a paradigm shift. It requires the gardener to view the landscape with a different lens. By this I mean that the gardener needs to begin looking at the entire landscape as one big picture—encompassing both her individual garden and the surrounding areas, because every decision and action in the home garden affects other aspects of the broader landscape. Fertilizers and chemicals that are soluble in water find their way into streams and freshwater sources and nitrogen applied to a backyard in Illinois may eventually end up in the Gulf of Mexico. If we want to reverse the trend of pollution we must begin to look at the big picture and shift to an attitude of proactive prevention rather than reactive attack. We must realize that what we do at home creates effects downstream.

If organic gardening requires a paradigm shift for most people, part of that shift involves thinking about our impact on the natural world. Plants produce fresh air, food for humans and wildlife, and build soil carbon. The organic paradigm requires critical thinking, including understanding the ways organic gardeners can minimize their negative impact on the planet while maximizing their positive impact.

Planting native plants—a standard organic practice—is an example of this. Native plants feed native animals, from insects to birds, from rabbits to hawks. Encouraging native plants in our gardens helps build the trophic base for all other higher organisms to live. While planting natives doesn't provide food on the dinner table (a big reason many people grow organic), it does impact the health of pollinators, soil microorganisms, and other wildlife, and this in turn impacts your vegetable garden.

Other aspects of the paradigm shift involve consumerism—the way we view needs versus wants. Recycling or repurposing is a natural part of gardening, as gardens are constantly in a state of change. A garden is a place of continual birth, growth, and death. Perennial and woody plants live to grow, reproduce, and then rest until the next season comes. Annual plants and flowers are nothing but showy organisms that attract pollinators, ensuring that the plants' seed is set and distributed before they die and return their biomass to the earth. When we add recycled or repurposed items to our gardens, we breathe new life into something that was otherwise destined for a landfill. This repurposing adds character to the garden and saves money.

The organic lifestyle is one that places a premium on reusing, repurposing, upcycling, and recycling.

❧ AMASSING SOIL CARBON

Soil carbon builds up over time as plant roots grow and die back in soil, and as microbes multiply and die in soil. These natural processes build soil carbon levels. Adding compost and organic matter helps accelerate the process because compost adds carbon and encourages the growth of microbes and roots.

Differences Between Organic and Conventional Gardening

Any type of gardening connects people to nature, but organic gardening connects people to nature more intensely because of the focus on building local biodiversity and abundance of life. The alternative to organic gardening, conventional gardening, involves the use of synthetic chemicals to control aspects of the garden, including pesticides to control weeds, insects, and diseases, and the use of synthetic chemical fertilizers applied to soil to encourage plant growth. The differences between the two approaches are quite clear when you look at the basic practices of using pesticides and fertilizers.

△ ▽ Leave annuals and perennials standing to provide food and shelter for wildlife during the winter.

PESTICIDES

Organic gardeners and farmers do, in fact, also use pesticides to control weeds, insects, and diseases. Common perception may be that organic growers use no pesticides whatsoever, but this is rarely true. The pesticides used in organic practices are generally less broadly toxic to soil, water, and air quality when used as directed on the label. However, some natural pesticides used in organic gardens can be toxic if used incorrectly or at incorrect quantities.

All pesticides—both synthetic and so-called organic pesticides—leave residues. How else would they work on pests? Chronic exposure to any pesticide can have negative health impacts. Pesticides—even organic pesticides—are toxic and can have unintended consequences that harm non-target pests. Even though a pesticide may be applied to a specific crop for a particular pest, if that pesticide washes into nearby sources of freshwater, it can have detrimental effects on aquatic life or wipe out a population of beneficial insects.

Pesticide exposure, including residues remaining on food consumed by humans, may contribute to a number of negative health conditions, including acute poisoning, leukemia, cancer, respiratory damage, neurological effects, and problems with the reproductive system. Repeated direct exposure exacerbates most of these conditions. While it may take a lifetime of ingesting small amounts of pesticide residue to induce one of these conditions, those who choose to garden with refined, synthetic chemicals and pesticides expose themselves to a much greater concentration of these chemicals than organic gardeners.

Using pesticides should always be an action of last resort for all gardeners rather than the first response. This is why I say organic gardening is part of a paradigm. It requires gardeners to shift their way of thinking to take the entire picture into account. You can't really call yourself a proponent of organic gardening, then still choose to spray any insect that moves in the garden, justifying the action because you're using something that's labeled "organic."

The unspoken covenant for an organic gardener is to take personal responsibility for how we use these chemicals. Owning this lifestyle ensures we keep ourselves healthy by limiting exposure to dangerous pesticides and ensures we aren't limiting the ability of future generations to grow food, drink water, and breathe air. Your paradigm shift will involve redefining what is an acceptable amount of plant damage before treatment with pesticides is warranted. Gardeners who minimize the use of pesticides soon find, though, that gardens stabilize in a way that keeps most pests to a minimum as the ecosystem becomes more natural. Lady bugs arrive to eat the aphids; song birds arrive to feast on cabbage worms.

Pesticide use or non-use is an important theme in the organic lifestyle, as it has the potential to improve or corrode the very world we live in.

FERTILIZERS

The greatest threat (and our greatest opportunity) to growing food lies in the health of the soil. When soils are degraded, it can take millennia to bring them back to the productivity they provided before chemical intervention.

Synthetic chemical fertilizers are, essentially, salts. Applying chemical fertilizer salts to soil over the course of many years changes the soil profile in many destructive ways. Salts accumulate in the soil, breaking apart the essentially healthy soil structure. Salts also impact soil microbial life, reducing population size and diversity. Organic soils can host a diverse and abundant variety of microbial species, but chemically fertilized soils have a different microbial profile, one that is much narrower than that of their organic counterparts. The fertilizer salts dry out soil and can prevent certain microbial communities from establishing or thriving because they place limitations on how these microbes live and reproduce. Synthetic chemical fertilizers have the potential to degrade soil quality by decreasing water-holding capacity and increasing the potential for erosion. In the long run, produce yields decrease on degraded soils.

COMPARATIVE RESEARCH

Increasing yield is the primary goal of all farms and backyard gardeners. Much has been written regarding the ability of organic versus conventional agriculture and which method has higher yields. Conventional agriculture proponents maintain that their yields are higher than those of organic systems, and while this may be true for some comparisons, there is scientific research that refutes these claims.

In southeast Pennsylvania, we are fortunate to be in the backyard of The Rodale Institute, which was established in 1947 by J. I. Rodale to research organic growing methods to benefit farms and gardeners everywhere. In 2011, the Institute

△ Sustainable management practices lead to long-term, abundant yields on organic farms.

completed a 30-year farming systems trial comparing conventional farming to organic farming methods. Results showed conclusively that organic yields can and did outcompete conventional counterparts. The first few years of data favored conventional agriculture; however, after the initial years, organic yields surpassed conventional yields and continued to increase with time. Organic methods offer a long-term advantage, not instant gratification.

Nature is unpredictable. Droughts, floods, insect plagues, storms, and other hazards have existed since agriculture began and seem to be occurring ever more regularly. The organic systems trial at Rodale proved that organic agriculture is more resilient to these extremes. In a world where climate events are unpredictable, resiliency is paramount to food security. Organic farms have the most impact on preserving soil quality and improving soil health because they control millions of agricultural acres in the US alone.

Personal Health Benefits of Going Organic

While the actions of organic farms have the most impact on national and global food systems, we cannot discount the impact of organic home gardeners. Organic gardens provide ecosystem benefits by providing food for many trophic levels in nature. Organic gardens provide a refuge for many forms of life, from microbial species in the soil to insects, birds, and other wildlife that live in or visit the garden, and ultimately give us produce to eat. An organic garden is alive with the sounds of nature and can feel like an oasis amidst gardens controlled by chemicals.

△ Insects flock to organic gardens and farms, which is a good thing. Beneficial insects are important pollinators. They also keep harmful insect populations in check.

There are several goals to aim for in an organic garden:

- Organic gardens should positively encourage environmental feedback loops. They should build soil health and productivity.

- They should help absorb water and nutrients. They should filter pollutants and other potential contaminates from reaching sources of freshwater.

- They should contribute to producing fresh air for all to breathe and enjoy.

- They should build the primary plant trophic level to feed insects and higher trophic levels (including humans).

- They should be places of replenishment for the body and soul. Gardens connect us to the natural world. Few things on this planet can do what gardens do. Many would argue there is no better way to spend your extra time than to be in a garden.

Like most forms of gardening and outdoor activity, organic gardening requires a moderate level of exercise, and this routine exercise in itself provides many health benefits, including lowering blood pressure, easing tension, reducing stress, increasing mental clarity, and raising feelings of accomplishment in the reward center of the brain. Gardening can also elevate your property value, reduce money spent on groceries, and increase biodiversity in your yard.

Not only does organic gardening provide a host of physical health benefits, but it also provides the gardener with food—provided that a veggie garden is part of the picture. Most proponents of organic gardening maintain that organically grown or produced foods contain more nutrition or beneficial compounds than their conventionally grown counterparts, though naturally this position is disputed by some advocates of the synthetic chemical approach. As is often the case with research, some studies can be cited that support either position, though it appears that the greater productivity of organic gardening becomes more apparent with longer periods of study. As the Rodale research cited earlier suggests, the merit of an organic lifestyle is not instant gratification, but long-term improvement.

A recently compiled meta-analysis of data comparing nutritional content of organic versus non-organic food shows that organically produced milk and meat contain higher levels of Omega-3 fatty acids. Organic crops, such as apples, blueberries, carrots, and broccoli, contain higher levels of antioxidants. Meat and dairy gains were achieved by feeding animals grass, which contains more Omega-3s than typical cattle feed, such as corn or silage.

Why is this so? Organic crops have to work harder to grow and thrive, and as a side effect they produce more self-defense compounds that are detrimental to insects and pathogens—compounds that are also beneficial to human and animal health.

Organically grown crops have been documented to contain higher levels of *anthocyanins*, the compounds that give plants (and fall leaves) their alluring shades

△ Organically grown produce will usually have some pest damage, but will still taste delicious.

◁ Visiting gardens is a great way to relieve stress.

◁ Scientific studies point to health benefits of spending time in nature, including the Japanese practice of "forest bathing."

🌿 FOREST BATHING

Being present in your organic garden during the magical time of early morning when beams of sunlight cascade through the trees onto you is akin to the practice of forest bathing. If you're not familiar with the concept of forest bathing, or *Shinrin-yoku*, as it's called in Japan, it involves (clothed) trips to the forest to "bathe" in sunlight as it shines through branches onto the forest floor.

Researchers in Japan and South Korea have conducted studies proving the health benefits of spending time under a forest canopy relaxing and enjoying nature. The benefits are similar to all proven benefits of being outside, working in the fresh air of the garden. Actively performing this method of relaxation would arguably be more effective in an organic garden than in a sterilized garden full of pesticides. Spending time unplugged from the daily presence of technology provides time for internal contemplation—reflecting on the past, present, and future of our lives.

of reds, oranges, and yellows. Anthocyanins have anti-inflammatory effects when consumed, and help protect our cells from degradation. The health benefits of eating organic have been scientifically proven, though the personal health benefits are only one of the many reasons why organic gardening supports healthy ecosystems.

Evidence from comparison studies of the shelf life of organic versus conventional produce suggests that organic produce lasts longer. Lower levels of nitrates in organic food and higher levels of naturally produced antioxidants likely contribute to the longer shelf life. Increased levels of antioxidants also are likely contributors to the improved flavor factor when comparing organic with conventional produce. In many studies, people rated organic produce as tastier than the same fruit or vegetable grown conventionally.

This should come with a caveat, which is that not all organic growers are created equal, just as not all conventional growers are created equal. There are some organic growers that do not take extra care when harvesting, delivering to market bruised or blemished produce that will deteriorate quickly. (Any injury on a piece of produce is an entry point for a pest or pathogen.) Bruised produce also emits ethylene, the same gas that helps bananas ripen, and this will cause bruised fruit to deteriorate faster than non-bruised fruit.

Health benefits aside, be aware that organically grown fruits and vegetables may not look as pretty as their conventionally grown counterparts. Some fruit may have tiny blemishes from insect damage. Some leafy greens may have a hole or two in them—or even an insect or two *on* them—due to the limited use of pesticides during their growth. Remember, organic farms have some pesticides at their disposal to help protect plants from insect outbreak; however, these pesticides are usually used as a case of last resort and generally have lower toxicity rates as compared to pesticides used on conventional farms.

Organic gardening is not exclusive to the great outdoors—it also reaches inside to houseplants. All plants can be maintained organically without worry of introducing potentially hazardous chemicals indoors. By using organic potting soil, fertilizer, and pest-control methods, all houseplants can be part of the organic gardening experience.

Beyond the Garden

Being organically minded while gardening organically involves adopting concepts within concepts—the definition of a true paradigm shift. Being organically minded means taking a whole-systems approach to everything in your life. It means you choose to walk rather than drive when possible; to take your reusable shopping bags to the grocery store; to choose fruit over a sugar-coated pastry; and to choose to shop at the local farmers' market instead of buying produce that was grown thousands of miles away from your grocery store.

Organically minded consumerism attempts to limit impact on the environment at every level. With this mindset, your garden will take on a whole new level of meaning and influence. Any amount of organic gardening helps to positively impact your garden, your ecosystem, and your local community. Just because you have to drive to work every day doesn't mean you can't strive to be more organically minded on each of those days. Every step is a step in the right direction, and each step in an organic direction is an achievement. Methodical change comes slowly, but incremental change can have wide-reaching effects over time.

This book details the major aspects of gardening organically for gardeners of all skill levels. It provides an overview of topics to the organic lifestyle, providing a framework that will help you develop a baseline of knowledge that in turn prepares you to go out and learn by practical experience.

At its basic level, gardening organically creates less work for the gardener by allowing nature to take its course. When you begin to think the way nature "thinks," your transformation to organic gardener is complete. When you tackle aspects or problems of the garden by thinking, "What would nature do?" you have now accepted the paradigm shift. Once you do, there's no going back!

△ (left) The home landscape in winter while the landscape lies dormant waiting for spring.

△ (right) The home landscape in mid-spring with grains growing alongside flowers in a diverse landscape/foodscape.

◁ The home landscape in fall showing an abundant fall grain harvest.

02

It All Begins with Soil: Organic Gardening from the Bottom Up

Soil is one of the most precious resources we have on this planet, yet most people don't even fully understand what is meant by the term "soil." Rather than being dismissed as mere "dirt," soil is actually a complex combination of solid mineral particles, organic matter, air, and water that together form a medium that establishes the base of the terrestrial food chain.

The mineral portion of soil includes, essentially, fine particles of ground-up rock minerals. It is formed over the course of millennia as the Earth's crust weathers via physical processes. Essentially, rocks break down and create soil. Soil properties differ based on the underlying parent bedrock material and environmental conditions present during soil formation, giving rise to the native soil of a location. This is what makes dark black Iowa topsoil different from the red soil of Georgia. Plant a seed in good soil and that seed will grow and thrive as long as Mother Nature provides sunlight and rain.

◁ Healthy soil is the foundation of all organic gardening.

The Science of Soil Layers

Soils are identified and analyzed by studying samples of them in profile—a cross-section of soil taken starting at the surface and extending down to the bedrock. The depth of the soil profile is directly related to the parent mineral material and the environmental conditions.

The soil profile is divided into layers, called *horizons*, which demarcate areas of nutrient accumulation or loss due to natural activity over time. The uppermost layer is the *O horizon*, referring to the organic material present. The organic material here is mostly vegetative material in a raw state or in the early stages of decomposition. For example, the duff layer of leaves, stems, and so forth on the forest floor is an O horizon layer.

Just underneath the O horizon is the *A horizon*, which is commonly known as topsoil. The A Horizon contains the bulk of soil nutrients and microbes, and is where most plant roots are found. Over time, this horizon loses certain substances (including nutrients) due to rain percolating through soil, a process known as *eluviation.* The downward movement of water pulls iron, aluminum, clay particles, organic matter, and other soluble compounds deeper into soil, into the next soil horizon, known as the *B horizon.* The B horizon is commonly referred to as *subsoil* and contains the iron, aluminum, clay particles, organic matter, and other soluble compounds that washed out of the A horizon. For ease of discussion purposes, in this book I'll refer to the A horizon as topsoil and the B horizon as subsoil.

While we rarely dig into it as gardeners, under the subsoil is a layer called the *C horizon.* This layer is composed of unconsolidated layers of rock, formed as the

COMPONENTS OF SOIL

▷ Soil is more than just solid mineral particles. It is an ecosystem complete with tiny organisms, bits of organic matter, reservoirs of water, air spaces, as well as the mineral "dirt" particles.

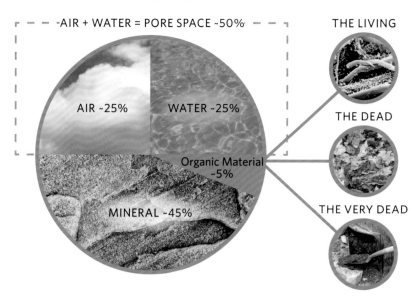

AIR + WATER = PORE SPACE ~50%

AIR ~25%

WATER ~25%

Organic Material ~5%

MINERAL ~45%

THE LIVING

THE DEAD

THE VERY DEAD

R horizon directly below it weathers over time. This layer may be permeable by a shovel, but will seem rocky and much different than the subsoil above it. Depending on climatic conditions, this layer may also hold soluble compounds from the layers above. The final layer is the *R horizon*, or bedrock. The depth of these horizons (layers) is different from region to region and changes based on the type of natural vegetation present, the climatic conditions, and the parent bedrock material. To the naked eye, these horizons are typically visibly pronounced by different colors.

The Importance of Soil

Soil has multiple functions in the garden. Without good, healthy soil, we cannot grow plants. Soil is a substrate for roots, which, in turn, support a plant's aboveground growth. Soil holds water and nutrients for plants; it is home to the microbes and soil animals responsible for nutrient cycling; and it acts as a filter for pollutants as water moves through the soil profile. Depending on environmental conditions, nutrients are either held in soil or released into the atmosphere. Soil has physical, chemical, and biological properties that affect plant performance in the landscape.

Physical Properties of Soil

We'll start by looking at physical properties, as they are dictated by soil texture (soil type). From the gardener's perspective, these are the least changeable properties of garden soil.

SOIL MINERAL COMPONENTS

Soil is made up of sand, silt, and clay particles. *Sand* is the largest of these particles, weighimg in at 2mm to 0.5mm in diameter. *Silt* particles are larger than clay particles, ranging in size from 0.5mm to .002mm. *Clay* particles are less than 0.002mm in diameter. Sandy soils feel coarse and gritty when rubbed between two

SOIL HORIZONS

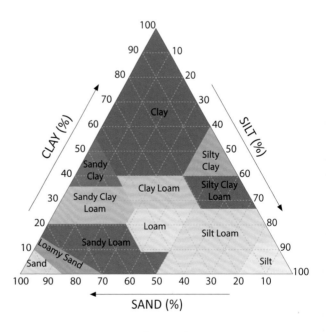

O (Organic)
A (Surface)

B (Subsoil)

C (Substratum)

R (Bedrock)

△ Geography, precipitation, and vegetation are all factors that contribute to the characteristics of an individual soil's layers, or horizons.

△ The texture of the soil influences drainage, nutrient retention, ease of tilling, and oxygen retention.

△ At a basic level, soil supports plants' roots. It is also a source of minerals, nutrients, and oxygen.

fingers. Silty soils feel like baking flour, while clay soils feel slippery. Sandy soils are very well drained—sometimes too well drained. The more clay or silt in your soil, the greater the moisture-holding capacity. But a poor soil indeed is one with too much clay, as water does not permeate at all and can drown plants growing in it.

Soils are often described according to the predominant particles they contain. A "sandy soil" is one where the percentage of coarse sand particles is greatest; "silty" or "clayey" soils, on the other hand, are those dominated by silt or clay particles, respectively.

An optimum garden soil is one called *loam*. Loam is usually defined as soil with roughly 40 percent sand, 40 percent silt, and 20 percent clay, and is regarded as ideal for growing most plants. However, native plants are very often already adapted to the soil types in a particular region, so some consideration needs to go into any decision to try to alter soils in a wholesale way.

A gardener's challenge, if faced with a soil that is extreme at either end of the scale, is to nudge it toward a more even mixture of coarser particles for better drainage and finer particles or other materials for moisture retention.

Soil type is based on the percentage of each of the three primary mineral particles in soil. You can use the soil texture triangle (see page 23) to determine your garden's soil type. There are 12 types, ranging from sandy soil to clay soil, silty clay to loam. The center of this soil textural triangle is the "holy grail" for gardeners.

HOW TO IMPROVE CLAY AND/OR SANDY SOIL

Gardeners experience issues when gardening in extreme soil types. Sandy soils do not hold nutrients or water as well as silt or clay do. If you garden in clay soil, you experience the opposite problem—dealing with highly moisture-retentive soil that

△ Biochar

△ Compost

may also be difficult to dig into and/or may be compacted. I find adding organic material in the form of compost is the best soil amendment for these extreme soil types, but it also improves any soil type, even the best loams. Compost can help increase the moisture- and nutrient-holding capacity in sandy soils, and will help drainage in clay-based soils.

I prefer compost over other soil amendments because high-quality compost contains loads of beneficial biology in addition to organic matter. Biochar can also be used to improve soil conditions (see Chapter 4).

SOIL TYPE VERSUS SOIL CLASSIFICATION

You can look up your local soil type online using United States Geological Survey (USGS) references (websoilsurvey.sc.egov.usda.gov/App/HomePage.htm), or by using an app called SoilWeb. Enter your location into SoilWeb and it will provide your soil type based on USGS records. Accuracy is currently within 100 meters, so odds are it will be pretty accurate for your location. Soil classifications are divided

SOIL ORDERS	CHARACTERISTICS	REGIONS OF THE US
Alfisol	Lower fertility than Mollisols, but still productive soil. Common under deciduous forest.	Great Lakes, Mississippi River Basin
Andisol	Developed from volcanic materials. High mineral content.	Parts of Pacific NW, Hawaii, and Alaska
Aridisol	Dry soils. Arid to semi-arid environments. Typically small O horizon.	Southwest
Entisol	Young soil, with little horizon distinctions. Common in urban soil.	Western plains, surrounded by Mollisols and Aridisols
Gelisol	Soils with permafrost. Cold or frozen most of the year.	Alaska
Histosol	Organic soils. High moisture-holding capacity. Low porosity. Commonly found in wetlands.	Northern Great Lakes and Outer Banks in NC
Inceptisol	Young soil, but with B horizon developing clearly. Older than Entisols.	Appalachia, and parts of Pacific NW
Mollisol	Great physical properties. Usually under grasslands. Fertile, well developed A horizon.	Midwest, Great Plains
Oxisol	Highly weathered. Organic matter mostly oxidized out of soil. Most common under old tropical forest.	Not prevalent in the US
Spodosol	Coarse-textured soil with lower fertility. Nutrient layer accumulates in or between A and B layers.	Parts of Florida and New England
Ultisol	Highly weathered soil, but more fertile than Oxisols. Common under tropical forest areas. Lower fertility.	Southeast and Northern Mid-Atlantic
Vertisol	Soil expands and contracts due to high clay content.	Parts of Texas and the South, along rivers

into orders with scientific-sounding names, such as Histosols, Mollisols, and Entisols. These names refer to the current soil conditions and/or the conditions under which they were created. From a gardener's perspective, soil type—sandy loam, clay soil, and so on—is more important than soil classification, as soil type is what indicates the soil management techniques that should be applied to maximize garden performance.

Chemical Properties of Soil

Chemical properties of soil include pH, salinity, cation exchange capacity (CEC), anion exchange capacity (AEC), organic matter, and carbon to nitrogen (C:N) ratio.

pH, SALINITY, AEC, AND CEC

Soil pH is a scale that measures the alkalinity and acidity levels of soil, which is determined by the number of hydrogen ions in soil. In practical terms, pH is an indicator of nutrient availability in soil.

Soil salinity refers to the amount of salts (fertilizers and nutrient content) present. These salts are measured by electrical conductivity (EC) present in the soil solution.

AEC refers to the soil's ability to hold and exchange negatively charged nutrients, such as nitrogen, phosphorus, sulfur, and chlorine. Soil must have positively charged sites available to attract and hold these negatively charged nutrients. AEC is greater at lower pH values, especially below 5.0. AEC decreases with increasing pH. In general, most soils have a low AEC, which means they can be subject to

THE BENEFITS OF USING HUMIC ACIDS IN SANDY SOILS

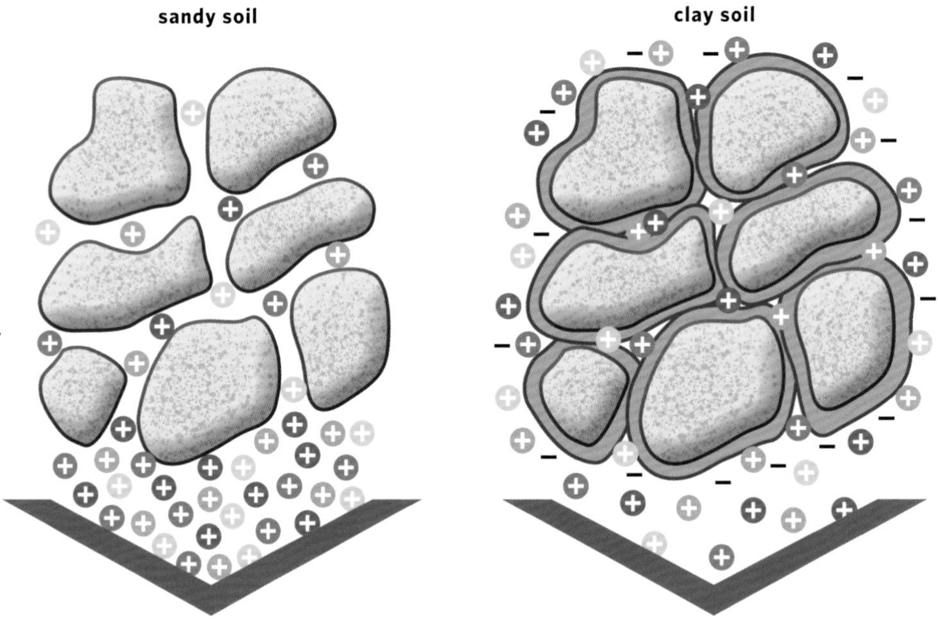

sandy soil

clay soil

▷ Soil particles hold on to or let go of nutrients. Clay soils cling to nutrients more tightly, while sandy soils leach (or let go of) nutrients.

❧ Practical Organic Gardening

leaching important plant nutrients, including nitrogen and phosphorus, and then require more frequent fertilizer or compost application.

CEC refers to the soil's ability to hold and exchange positively charged nutrients, such as ammonium, potassium, calcium, magnesium, iron, zinc, copper, sodium, and hydrogen. Clays have significant impact on chemical properties of soil, especially CEC. At the microscopic level, clays are made up of platelets with many negatively charged sites; these negatively charged sites attract the positively charged nutrients, resulting in the two binding together to hold nutrients in soil. Compost and biochar also have CEC and AEC, and can hold nutrients in the soil profile. That is why applying compost and biochar can improve nutrient capacity in soils. CEC increases as soil pH increases.

Dominant Soil Texture	Average CEC
Sandy soil	3-15
Silty soil	10-30
Clay soil	20-50
Organic soil	50+
Potting soil	75+

ORGANIC MATTER

Organic matter in the soil increases CEC, increases resistance to changes in soil pH, and helps microbes break down soil minerals. It consists of plant residues (roots, leaves, and so on), actively decomposing materials (*detritus*), and stable organic materials that have undergone decomposition (*humus*).

Most soils contain between 3 to 6 percent organic matter, with 5 percent being the target for most garden soils. Ten-percent organic matter is not uncommon in more intensively managed soils, such as those in a vegetable garden. Organic matter in soil also provides an important food source for microbes, and helps create soil structure to increase water infiltration and storage.

◁ Soils high in organic matter readily retain moisture and nutrients, while soils low in organic matter tend to drain quickly and leach nutrients.

C:N RATIO

C:N ratio refers to the ratio of *carbon* molecules to *nitrogen* molecules present in soil, and is used as an indicator of soil or compost quality. A high C:N means there will be less nitrogen available for plant roots. A low C:N ratio indicates degraded organic materials and greater nitrogen availability. Compost with a low C:N ratio is better for gardens, because any C:N ratio higher than 20:1 indicates the compost is not yet completely mature. Most soil tests do not include a C:N ratio—however, any good compost test will include a C:N ratio to show the ability of the compost to provide nitrogen once incorporated into soil.

Biological Properties of Soil

Soil contains sand, silt, clay, and organic matter, but it also contains a living biological quotient, which in healthy soil is an incredibly diverse and abundant population. Soil organisms include microscopic animals such as bacteria, protozoa, fungi, nematodes, rotifers, and other small soil-dwelling organisms, but also larger animals such as springtails, arachnids, and earthworms. These organisms help break down organic matter and add to soil nutrient content. One teaspoon can contain up to a billion bacteria, thousands of linear feet of fungi, thousands of protozoa, and dozens of nematodes—and that's just the microbiology we can't see with the naked eye!

Soil organisms are constantly breeding, eating and being eaten, and driving the soil nutrient-cycling forward. When we enhance soil biology by adding compost and other organic materials, we also increase species diversity and abundance. Biological soil components are important because they're involved in disease suppression potential and nutrient cycling, among other things. Here's how the different biological organisms contribute to the soil.

BACTERIA

Bacteria are single-celled organisms at the base of the food chain, and they provide the bulk of soil-available nitrogen in an organic garden. Bacteria called *actinomycetes* give soil that classic earthy smell, like a garden in springtime. Bacteria help protect plant roots from pathogens and produce many valuable compounds in the root zone.

FUNGI

Fungi are vital soil inhabitants responsible for nutrient cycling, soil remediation, and linking vast swaths of soil (and plants) together. Within the fungi category are the *mycorrhizal* fungi. Mycorrhizae form a symbiotic relationship with plant roots. They connect with plants by growing directly into or between cells along plant roots and exchanging carbon (energy) for nutrients and water. The mycorrhizal fungi extend a plant's rooting area dramatically and funnel nutrients and water back to the plant. In exchange, the plant gives the fungus sugars (carbon) to use as an energy source, as fungi lack chlorophyll, the necessary green pigment in leaves that allows a plant to harvest the sun's energy and convert it into sugars.

Only a biological soil test can tell you the quantity and diversity of these organisms present in your soil. I like to think of soil biology as an underground safari. Within the soil, organisms are constantly getting eaten and struggling to survive. Smaller organisms are prey and larger organisms are the hunters.

PROTOZOA

Protozoa are larger single-celled organisms, and analysis of them can indicate whether a soil is aerobic (containing oxygen) or anaerobic (lacking oxygen), depending on the type present. Protozoa are the amoeba-shaped animals that cruise through soil looking for bacteria to eat. The C:N ratio of bacteria is less than the C:N ratio of the amoeba. Because the C:N ratio is comparatively less in the bacteria, not all the nitrogen is required by the amoeba to live. The amoeba exudes excess soluble nitrogen absorbed from the bacteria through its cell wall. This water-soluble nitrogen can then be taken up by plant roots or used as food by other microbes.

FISHING FUNGI

The safari doesn't end with bacteria and amoeba! There are fungi that create loops as they grow, in the hopes that a nematode will swim through the loop. In a split second, the loop tightens around the nematode and traps it in the grasp of the fungus. The fungus produces enzymes that break down the nematode into nutrients. The fungus can then absorb the nutrients into its body and the cycle continues. Not all the nutrients are absorbed by the "fishing" fungus, and some of the nutrients are absorbed by other soil-dwelling organisms, by nearby plant roots, or absorbed back into the soil nutrient bank.

△ Fungi

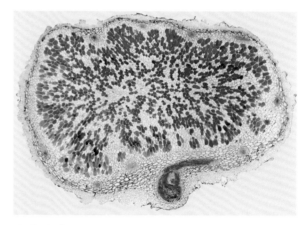
△ Bacteria

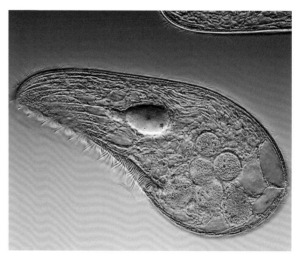
△ Protozoa

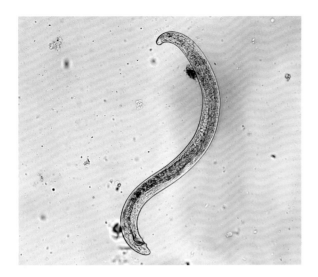

△ Nematode

△ Root-feeding nematode

NEMATODES

Then there are the nematodes. Nematodes are microscopic organisms that are long and cylindrical in shape with a wormlike appearance (they are nonsegmented roundworms, technically). Nematodes can be beneficial or parasitic.

Beneficial nematodes protect plants by infecting insects and eating pathogens. In essence, the process is something like this: a nematode enters a host insect through any given opening or directly through the cell walls. Its secret weapon is the bacteria that live in the nematode's gut. The nematode "pukes up" the bacteria while inside the host insect. The bacteria begin to multiply and produce compounds that poison the host and turn the host body to a hot mess of insect goo—which is in turn eaten by the nematode, which then proceeds to multiply over and over due to the abundance of food. The cycle continues until all the food is gone, then the new nematodes burst forth to enter the soil solution and repeat the cycle.

But parasitic nematodes cause destruction of plant leaves and roots. Root-feeding nematodes are common in certain parts of America. One such example is the root-knot nematode, which infects roots and stunts growth, giving the roots a knotted appearance. While root-knot nematodes are typically a problem in areas with hot growing seasons and mild winters, scientists at Cornell University have identified a species of northern root-feeding nematodes in New York soils.

HOW MICROBES FIND PLANTS IN THE SEA OF SOIL

Microbes can sense food sources in the soil. I call this the "cookies in the kitchen" effect. Utilizing pheromones, microbes can "smell" the carbon coming off plant roots growing in the soil. The growing root tip is constantly sloughing off cells, which provide surplus sugars, amino acids, cellulose, pectin, starch, and lignin—all different types of carbon—for microbes to eat. Once they find the root zone, microbes sense whether the habitat is ideal for them or not. If ideal, they take up residence with the roots.

Every root has what are called root hairs that extend from the root in search of water and nutrients. Root hairs are the primary locations of water and nutrient uptake in plants. To the naked eye, these root hairs look like a seamless extension of the plant root.

Under a microscope, however, we see root hairs emerging from a larger structural root. Cracks around the edges of where the root hair emerges are quickly filled in by microbes, which establish budding communities, as there is plenty of food (in the form of root exudates, such as cellulose) available at the root/root hair interface. Pathogens can also enter the same cracks and infect the root, but when beneficial microbes are present in abundant quantities, they fill these spaces quickly to help the plant block disease.

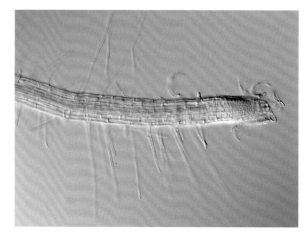

△ Root hairs are the primary point of entry for nutrients and water, as well as a colonization site for microbes.

Garden Soil Versus Potting Soil

When this topic comes up, people often ask me, "Isn't garden soil the same as potting soil?" The short answer is that they are not the same thing at all.

Potting soil is not simply soil dug up in the backyard and placed in a pot. In fact, the term "potting soil" is a bit of a misnomer, in that potting soil is a soilless medium, without any actual sand, silt, or clay in it at all. Potting soil is typically made of peat moss, composted bark, and perlite—not garden soil.

Other bulk ingredients found in potting soils include compost, coconut husk fiber, sand, vermiculite, rice hulls, and worm castings.

This list does not include any minerals or nutrients that should be added to potting soil, but we'll discuss minerals and nutrients in Chapter 4.

Potting soil serves several functions, just like soil, but potting soil is designed for use in container gardening. Potting soil provides ballast for plant roots to anchor and hold up the plant. It also provides storage for air, water, and nutrients. When shopping for a potting soil, make sure it's appropriate for the plant(s) you'll be potting. A tomato plant grows best in an all-purpose potting soil designed for outdoor use.

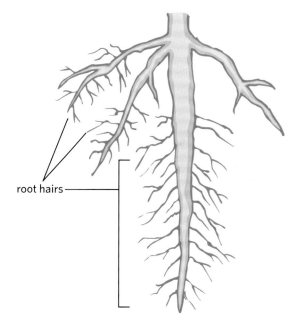

root hairs

△ Root hairs do much of the work when it comes to absorbing water and nutrients.

▷ Peat moss, aged bark, perlite, compost, coconut husk fiber, sand, vermiculite, rice hulls, worm castings

△ All-purpose potting soil

△ Cactus and succulent potting soil

Cactus and succulents, on the other hand, need a much different type of soil built to drain well.

It's best to visit your local garden center/plant shop when shopping for potting soil. You're guaranteed to find the best locally made products there. Check out the bag labels for details; that way you'll end up with the right soil for your needs.

 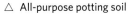

AREN'T ALL POTTING SOILS ORGANIC?

Short answer: no. Long answer: it's complicated.

Potting soils, while they are regulated by each state in the union, are not subject to any voluntary verification systems, and any company can slap the word "organic" on a bag of potting soil without any oversight. However, there are third-party verification programs out there. Currently, the most widely recognized certification for any gardening product is the OMRI listing.

Soil Testing

Before starting a new garden, one of the most important things to do is get the soil tested. That way you'll know what you're starting with and have a baseline for making decisions on how to handle your soil.

SOIL SAMPLING HOW-TO AND ANALYSIS

State extension offices usually have economical testing programs, including test kits for easy sample collection and submission. When testing soil, it's important to note a few rules. Make sure you are ordering the appropriate test. There are different types of testing for garden soil (Melich III, Bray-1, Olson P, or Modified Morgan extractable) versus potting soil (saturated paste extract).

All soil tests show you nutrient content present in soil; however, garden soil tests use an acid wash to strip soils of all nutrients, not just the water-soluble nutrients. A saturated paste test, on the other hand, confirms just the water-soluble nutrients present in the soil sample. Much of the nutrient content reported in an acid wash-type test is held too tightly in the soil and is therefore not available to plants. Further, it is not appropriate to compare test results produced by two different testing methods—to do so is equivalent to comparing apples to oranges.

Only take samples from the direct area in question. Example: If testing the soil in your veggie garden, only collect samples from inside the veggie garden

WHAT IS OMRI

When buying potting soil (or any garden input for that matter) look for one with the OMRI seal. OMRI is the Organic Materials Review Institute (www.omri.org), an independent third-party reviewer of inputs for organic farming. Soils, fertilizer, insect controls, plant growth enhancers, and more can be listed by OMRI if they meet the organization's strict standards. OMRI standards are based on the National Organic Program, the oversight committee responsible for setting standards for USDA-certified organic farms.

OMRI Listed® potting soils and fertilizers are tested for heavy metals, nutrient content, fecal coliform, and salmonella bacteria. Other OMRI requirements include zero tolerance for products directly produced with GMO ingredients, sewage sludge, or irradiated products: because these three are not allowed in organic agriculture, they are also not allowed in OMRI-listed products.

While OMRI is not ubiquitous in the gardening lexicon, it is gaining ground among organic gardeners as the go-to source for information on all things organic in the garden. Organic farms are very familiar with OMRI, because farms find that by sticking to OMRI-listed products they can simplify their record-keeping and input sourcing.

△ Look for the OMRI seal when shopping for organic garden amendments, fertilizers, and pest controls.

borders. Take samples from the top 2 to 6 inches of soil, but keep roots out of the sample soil. Collect at least three different samples from within the test area, with each sample approximately equidistant from the last. Collecting more samples gives you a better average result. Mix the samples together uniformly to create one sample for testing.

If you choose to order a soil test kit online, follow the directions that come in your test kit (or online instructions) and send in for testing. Once complete, the lab will send you results. Basic test results will show you the amount of nutrients present in your soil and will also include EC and pH measurements.

There are more detailed tests available, but the most relevant data is determined by testing for organic matter content (by percentage) and CEC (the ability to hold nutrients). The test result and analysis sent back to you will show the actual nutrient content present, the ideal range of nutrients present, and may also provide some guidance on how to get nutrients or pH into the ideal range based on the crops being grown. Methods and materials to amend soil to increase specific nutrient content are covered in Chapter 4.

RUNNING A SATURATED PASTE EXTRACT SOIL TEST AT HOME

You can run a basic version of the saturated paste extract at home, on potting soil or on garden soil, using the following process:

1. Collect your sample as described above and set it aside. You'll also need a pH/EC meter. These can be purchased online. Choose a professional-grade meter for best results.

2. Gather a large coffee filter, a funnel, a gallon of distilled water from the grocery store, and a plastic container. Fold the coffee filter in half, then fold it in half a second time. Pull open the folded filter to create a cone shape.

3. Insert the coffee filter cone in the funnel, then place your soil sample inside the cone. Place the funnel over the plastic container. The plastic container is in place to capture the saturated water solution.

4. Slowly add water to the soil in the funnel a shot at a time until the soil is saturated and shiny. Take your time with this process. Water should not begin dripping through for at least 30 minutes. After the soil is saturated, the water will begin to flow through the soil and into the receptacle.

5. Use a pH/EC meter to test the pH and salt content of the resulting liquid extract that drained out of the funnel. While this does not give you all the nutrient content details of your soil, it gives a quick and inexpensive indicator of fertility and pH.

SOIL pH

As expressed earlier, pH is a measure of the hydrogen ions in soil. In practical terms, it's an indicator of acidity or alkalinity.

Neutral pH is 7.0, the midpoint on the pH scale. Anything less than 7.0 is acidic and anything more than 7.0 is alkaline. Potting soils should be between 5.5 and 6.5 for most plants, and garden soil should be between 6.0 and 7.5. There are exceptions. Plants in the blueberry family (which includes azaleas, rhododendrons, and so on) like acidic soil, at or below pH 5.5.

Nutrients have to dissolve into the soil-water solution before plant roots can absorb them. The pH of the soil-water solution dictates how this process proceeds. If soil is too acidic, macronutrients such as nitrogen, phosphorus, and potassium are less available, but if it is too alkaline, micronutrients such as iron, copper, and manganese are less available. Any nutrient deficiency halts plant growth until the deficiency is fixed. Nutrients may be present in soil, but if pH is not ideal, the nutrients may not be available to plant roots.

AVERAGE pH	pH	COMMON ITEM
0	Acidic	Battery acid
1	^	Stomach acid
2	I	Lemon juice, vinegar
3	I	Soda, orange juice
4	I	Beer, wine
5	I	Bananas, black coffee
6	I	Urine, milk
7	Neutral	Distilled water
8	I	Eggs
9	I	Baking soda
10	I	Antacids
11	I	Ammonia solution
12	I	Soapy water
13	v	Bleach, oven cleaner
14	Alkaline	Liquid drain cleaner

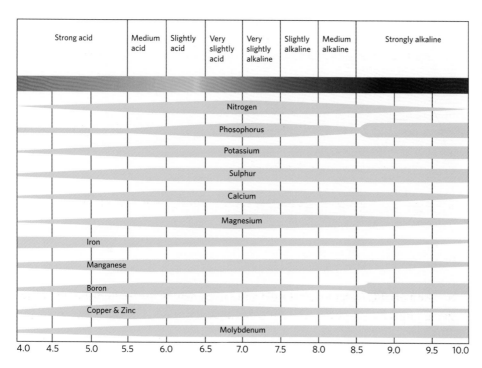

◁ The pH of the soil affects nutrient availability to plants. If the pH is off, it does no good to add fertilizer, as plants will not be able to use it.

△ Apply sulfur (top) to lower the pH and lime (bottom) to raise it.

Soil pH changes slowly over time. The pH of potting soil changes much quicker than the pH of garden soil, yet still takes time. Changing the pH of an aquaponic or hydroponic system is the fastest, because these systems are built on water-soluble nutrients. Any time you are starting a new garden is a good time to send samples off for testing and to make adjustments. Check for pH in garden soils approximately every three years until you have a good handle on your soil's pH range and variability. A hydroponic grower will check the pH of their nutrient solution much more frequently, sometimes on a daily basis, to ensure the plant has the nutrient solution it needs at an appropriate pH value.

MODIFYING SOIL pH

Native soil pH varies depending on where you live. The East Coast and Pacific Coast tend to have slightly acidic soil, while the Midwest has soil pH near neutral. Arid soils such as those found in the Rocky Mountains tend to be slightly alkaline.

We can modify pH by adding soil amendments. Ingredients such as pine fines, sulfur granules, iron sulfate, or aluminum sulfate can be used to lower pH. Garden lime (or dolomitic lime) is typically the best product to raise pH in soil. Make use of these products, which are readily available at your local garden center, if your test results come back outside the ideal pH range.

When using any product to amend pH of soil, always follow the directions on the label. Companies spend a lot of time researching the optimal application rates to achieve the desired goal, and the label is the best source of this information.

Be aware that plants themselves can change the pH of soil to a limited degree. Plant roots have a limited ability to change the pH microenvironment where the root zone interfaces with the surrounding soil-water solution. Roots can exude compounds that reduce or increase pH to a more favorable range in the microenvironment directly around the root zone, an area known as the *rhizosphere*. This pH adjustment makes nutrients more soluble and available for plant roots to uptake. If your soil test shows your pH is out of the ideal range, it's best to take action and not rely on the plant, which can only make limited changes to its microenvironment. Plants also vary in their ability to change pH, and as such we should take on the task of pH management.

Soil Fertility: The Big Picture

Soil fertility is based on the parent soil characteristics (soil structure and physical properties), organic matter, microbial community, and environmental conditions present (average weather patterns, rainfall, and so on). Fertility helps sustain plant growth. Soil with good microbial habitats will have increased soil fertility, due to the cumulative actions of soil microbes.

The process of mineralization also builds up the nutrient bank in soil. Nutrients help microbes live and multiply. The nutrient bank of soil fertility is constantly

DEFICIENCY OF MICRONUTRIENTS

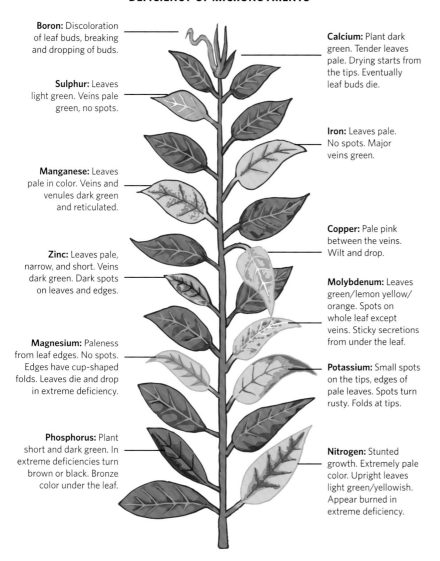

Boron: Discoloration of leaf buds, breaking and dropping of buds.

Sulphur: Leaves light green. Veins pale green, no spots.

Manganese: Leaves pale in color. Veins and venules dark green and reticulated.

Zinc: Leaves pale, narrow, and short. Veins dark green. Dark spots on leaves and edges.

Magnesium: Paleness from leaf edges. No spots. Edges have cup-shaped folds. Leaves die and drop in extreme deficiency.

Phosphorus: Plant short and dark green. In extreme deficiencies turn brown or black. Bronze color under the leaf.

Calcium: Plant dark green. Tender leaves pale. Drying starts from the tips. Eventually leaf buds die.

Iron: Leaves pale. No spots. Major veins green.

Copper: Pale pink between the veins. Wilt and drop.

Molybdenum: Leaves green/lemon yellow/ orange. Spots on whole leaf except veins. Sticky secretions from under the leaf.

Potassium: Small spots on the tips, edges of pale leaves. Spots turn rusty. Folds at tips.

Nitrogen: Stunted growth. Extremely pale color. Upright leaves light green/yellowish. Appear burned in extreme deficiency.

in flux due to microbial health, the addition of minerals and fertilizers, soil management practices, and the removal of soil nutrients by plant roots. Soil fertility is depleted as plants take up nutrients to grow, flower, and produce fruit. Tilling also reduces soil fertility as it speeds up oxidation of organic matter in soil.

To keep soil fertile and productive, we need to replace nutrients where they are not automatically replenished, such as in the vegetable garden, where most all the nutrients get removed each year, either in the form of harvested vegetables or plant mass removed and composted. In a perennial garden bed or in the forest, where some plants die back and others drop leaves and branches that feed the soil, not as much work is needed.

The next chapter will discuss organic methods for caring for soil in environmentally respectful ways.

03

Respecting the Soil Versus "Working" the Soil

Everything we do to the soil affects its ability to be productive, and as such, soil quality has been in peril ever since we started using mass quantities of chemicals (including pesticides) and extensively tilling soil in order to produce food. While this occurs on a large scale in commercial agriculture, chemical use and tilling happens in home gardens too. It all adds up.

Chemical use is a problem because it can cause salt accumulation in soils, changing the microbial environment in a way that inadvertently creates favorable conditions for the most *facultative* microbial species in soil—those that can survive in a variety of conditions. The opposite type of organisms—called *obligates*—require a specific set of conditions in order to thrive. The ultimate result is a decline in soil diversity. Upsetting that balance can affect plant growth.

◁ The key to good soil structure is to avoid overworking it.

Just as impactful as chemical use is constant tilling or working of the soil. It isn't just what we put into the soil that can change it, but how we work with the soil to control weeds, plant, and harvest. Obviously, you want the best soil for your organic garden. Here's what you need to know to work with the soil, not against it.

Soil Structure

Soil structure refers to the relationship between soil particles and the air spaces in soil. Good soil structure offers high water infiltration and, therefore, reduced erosion. When it rains, soil absorbs water quickly without much runoff. Soil cultivation damages soil structure by reducing pore spaces and breaking up larger soil chunks into smaller particles. With reduced pore spaces and smaller soil particles, the spaces fill with particles, which means there is no space for water to come in. Over time, this soil can become compacted to the point where plant growth slows due to reduced water infiltration and lack of pore space for air exchange.

Soil structure is improved over the course of time as aggregates form. Soil aggregates, also known as *soil peds*, are improved by microbial activity; freeze/thaw repetition; saturating and drying back out; root growth and resulting root death; and soil fauna (earthworms and other organisms). When soil is well aggregated, it has one of several distinct appearances.

Soil structure	Description
Blocky	Angular or sub-angular irregular blocky peds aggregated together
Columnar	Vertical columns of soil, rounded top, found in arid regions
Granular	Crumb-like, usually found near soil surface
Platy	Thin, horizontal flat plates of soil, usually compacted soils
Prismatic	Vertical columns of soil, flat top, found in lower levels of soil
Single grained	Individual soil particles that do not aggregate well, typical in sandy soil

Within each soil horizon there will be one type of aggregate or ped; however, there can be different types of aggregates in each of the soil horizons. Granular or crumb types are usually found in the A horizon, while the B horizon usually hosts blocky, columnar, or prismatic soil aggregation.

SOIL TILTH

Soil tilth is related to soil structure, and is an indication of workability and soil water-holding capacity. Every gardener wants soil with good tilth, because it means you can slide your shovel in the ground without resistance to plant something. Soil with good tilth has good soil structure, as it accepts water readily and resists erosion. You can tell that your soil has good tilth if, after turning over a shovel's worth of soil in the garden, the soil breaks up into aggregated soil peds but still seems chunky. If it's difficult to get your shovel in the ground, that's an indicator that your soil has reduced tilth.

The best ways to improve soil tilth include adding organic matter, cover cropping, reducing tillage, and planting more plants in general, especially annual or perennial plants that will put a lot of carbon in the soil as their roots grow and die back each year. Soils with good tilth have exceptional water-holding capacity because they have a variety of pore space sizes. Larger macro pores allow water infiltration, while smaller micro pores hold moisture that becomes accessible to roots in times of drought when larger pores are empty.

OXYGEN CONTENT IN THE SOIL

One of the key components of soil is the air space in between soil particles. This air space is crucial to plant health, as plant roots need to breathe. In plants, we call the breathing process respiration. When plant roots respire, they are taking in oxygen and exuding carbon dioxide. The opposite reaction occurs above ground in the leaves, where leaves take in carbon dioxide and release oxygen as part of the process of photosynthesis. The carbon dioxide reacts with water in cells, and the byproducts of this chemical reaction are glucose and oxygen. Because the plant does not need all the extra oxygen it produces, it exudes the extra oxygen through its leaves to feed our atmosphere (and allow us to breathe).

If we overcompact soil, we reduce or remove these important air spaces in the soil, but when we have sufficient air spaces in soil, oxygen and carbon dioxide can continually flow in and out of the root zone. Water helps displace carbon dioxide when it infiltrates the root zone, and brings fresh oxygen in behind it. If roots do not get enough oxygen, plant growth slows. If air space is severely limited, the plant may eventually die due to lack of oxygen and the ability to respire normally.

Every time we dig a hole or in any way dig into soil, we have the potential to reduce its air spaces. Next time you dig a hole to plant something, look critically at

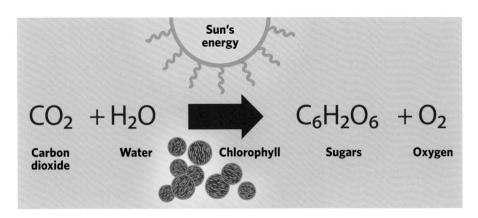

$$CO_2 + H_2O \rightarrow C_6H_2O_6 + O_2$$

Carbon dioxide   Water   Chlorophyll   Sugars   Oxygen

Sun's energy

△ The chemical equation for photosynthesis.

△ Pay attention to the soil structure when digging. Make adjustments when necessary.

the soil you're digging up. Hopefully you find a couple earthworms when digging, but you should also see air spaces in the soil. These will show up as small pockets of air in the soil at the edges or inside of larger soil chunks.

When working the hole to dig it out, you should see that the soil breaks up in chunks—larger chunks at first, but the more you dig, the smaller the soil particles will become. These soil chunks, or fragments, are called *soil clods*. While you can take this process too far with a shovel, reducing soil particle size is especially evident when tilling soil with a machine. When using a tiller, at first the chunks dug up are large, but after the second pass or so, the soil particles become quite small, affecting its long-term functionality.

Soil Conservation

One of the biggest threats to the soil is overworking it. You can't completely stay out of the soil, though. The very act of gardening means you will be digging it up and moving it around. Here's why less work equals more reward when it comes to the soil.

◁ Severe drought in combination with repetitive tilling led to the Dust Bowl conditions of the 1930s.

EFFECTS OF TILLING

While some soil is lost each year naturally through water or wind erosion, tillage results in far more soil being lost each year. The USDA has a term for soil lost at each tilling: the *T value*, or soil loss tolerance. The USDA maintains that the T value represents the acceptable amount of soil lost each year to erosion.

The biggest contributor to increasing T values is soil tillage, as most of the potential soil loss occurs during tilling, when soil particulates are literally blown away. It was excessive tilling that generated enough windborne soil to create the Dust Bowl in the United States in the 1930s. T values are unique from region to region, and are directly related to the soil type present in an area. T values range from 2 to 5 tons per acre per year and any loss of topsoil is a tragedy for future farmers and inhabitants of the planet, as it takes hundreds of years to build just one inch of topsoil.

Tillage degrades physical properties of soil by decreasing air space and reducing pathways for microbes to move through soil. Tilling increases erosion and nutrient losses, reduces the water-infiltration rate, and reduces populations of soil microbes and larger soil fauna. And, if that weren't enough, tilling also destroys soil structure, and creates a compacted hardpan layer under the tilling area.

WHEN TO USE A TILLER

Tilling can be appropriate when starting a new garden patch, planting a field for the first time, or working a particular problem soil that has been degraded over time. However, after the first year I advise against tilling in the home garden. If you are going to the expense and effort of tilling, it's important to get it done right the first time.

△ There are instances where the use of a tiller is warranted.

CONSERVATION TILLAGE

Farms employ a number of tilling methods and technologies. This process has been honed since large-scale agriculture began after the invention of the tractor. By and large, most farms today employ *intensive, reduced,* or *conservation* tillage.

If you regularly drive through agricultural farm lands, you may have noticed a change in tilling practices over the years. The sight of vast expanses of fields tilled smooth after the harvest is somewhat rare these days, as farmers more often leave fields intact in the months after harvest. When they do plow and till, the fields are left in somewhat rough shape, with plenty of plant material left in place. You may see a single pass of plowing as old plant material is turned over into the ground to feed the soil, but rarely do you see the extensive use of a tractor-pulled disc, tiller, and rake that once was common. This does not reflect laziness of today's farmers at all, but rather a deeper understanding of modern soil conservation strategies.

Intensive tillage is the most invasive, and leaves the least amount of crop residue on the soil surface. Reduced tillage leaves more plant residue on the soil surface, and helps reduce erosion. One form of conservation tillage is *zone tillage,* which involves deep tillage in narrow strips throughout the field. Zone tillage creates a seedbed for planting, helps soils warm faster and increase water infiltration—all without potential for extensive erosion. Zone tillage has been in use for almost 50 years, and is currently used on more than 30 percent of farmland, primarily in the Midwest.

PROS AND CONS OF SOIL TILLAGE

NO to LOW TILL—PROS	TILLING—CONS
Reduces soil erosion	Increases soil erosion
Maintains soil structure	Destroys soil structure
Uses less energy	Requires more energy inputs
Conserves water	Requires more irrigation
Reduces soil compaction	Sets up compacted hardpan layer

THE RIGHT WAY TO USE A TILLER

The less tilling, the better: tilling destroys soil structure and you now know why that is undesirable. If you are going to use a tiller, though, plan on making as few passes as possible while still getting the job done.

1. Mow down any vegetation present. You can do this with an actual lawn mower or with a string trimmer (weed whacker). Remove this vegetation if it contains weed seed. If it is only vegetation (if plants have not gone to seed), you can till it into the soil to add organic matter.

2. Till the area with a couple of passes, just enough to break up the existing soil.

3. Add any soil amendments across the entire garden area. (Of course, you've had the soil tested and know about any soil nutrient deficiencies, and have planned ahead by purchasing any soil amendments you need.)

Compost is the most common soil amendment to add—at least 2 to 4 inches of the good stuff—but your soil test results may also show a specific nutrient deficiency. It's easy to choose a soil amendment to fix, or remediate, any lacking nutrient. A trip to the local garden center or farm/feed store (not a big-box store) can provide a worthwhile learning experience to find a fertilizer that provides any missing nutrients. Share your garden project story with a knowledgeable staff member. They'll guide you to the organic fertilizer or mineral amendment you need to correct any nutrient deficiency in your soil.

REDUCING SOIL COMPACTION

Preserve the structure of your garden soil not only by limiting tillage, but also by limiting foot traffic, which can compact the soil. If plenty of volume and air space leads to good garden soil, any physical force that compacts the soil will be bad for it. In other words, your grandmother knew what she was talking about when she

▷ Steppingstones guide foot traffic and reduce soil compaction.

▽ Dig pathways between planting beds to elevate the bed height.

yelled, "Stay out of my garden beds!" when you were a child. Grandma was trying to keep you out of her beds so the soil would stay nice and fluffy.

After spending all that time and effort tilling all the compost and fertilizer into your new garden beds, the last thing you want to do is walk all over it. You'll notice how fluffy the soil is if you walk on it, as your foot will sink into the freshly prepared soil. Foot traffic compacts the soil again and reverses all the hard work you just did. This is especially problematic in the spring when gardeners are eager to get into the gardens and work the soil. Soil that is moist and just thawing is very susceptible to compaction and you can do severe damage by walking all over it in the early spring before it begins to dry out.

△ Walking in newly tilled soil immediately compacts it, reducing pore spaces and eliminating any structural improvements gained from tilling.

To avoid this compaction, make sure to carve paths into the garden bed. You can dig out pathways of tilled soil and shovel it onto the beds on either side of the walkway. This also increases the depth of your raised beds, creating more space for roots to grow.

Or, if you prefer, you can also use stepping stones to create garden bed paths. You can clear out soil pathways first, and then lay down the stepping stones, or just lay down stepping stones to create the garden paths. Placing stepping stones on top of the tilled soil will compact the soil slightly, but the large surface area of the stepping stone helps distribute the weight and force of your footprint across the entire surface of the stone. This results in less compaction because the force is evenly distributed.

Building New Garden Beds

When is the best time to build a new garden bed? Then answer is: whenever you want. As long as you can get a shovel in the ground, you can plant.

However, the ideal times are in the early spring after the ground thaws or in the fall before plants go to sleep for the winter. In summer, the ground is generally drier and harder than in spring or fall, and thus requires more work to create a new garden bed.

Spring and fall (or even winter if you live in a mild climate) are better times, because this is mostly when we receive the bulk of our rain. In spring the soil will thaw out as temperatures rise. At this time, the soil will be moist but not saturated. These conditions are ideal for digging, as moist soils are soft soils and should accept a tiller or shovel quite easily. The same conditions can be true in fall if you dig a new bed after the fall rains return, but before the cold of winter sets in.

If it's early spring and you're questioning if it's the right time to break ground in the veggie garden, try getting a shovel in the ground. If you can

 PROFESSIONAL TIP

Don't try to build a new garden bed immediately after heavy rains. If soil is saturated and you try to dig or till, you may end up destroying all the air space, as digging or tilling wet soil usually ends up making a muddy mess, removing all air space present. Give the soil a couple days to drain and dry out before digging or tilling.

△ Build new planting beds in the spring or the fall when soil is moist but not soggy.

△ Don't be fooled into thinking your soil needs to be ground into dust. Leaving the soil structure as is when you plant will ensure strong root establishment.

sink the shovel blade all the way into the ground, you can certainly work the soil. If the shovel blade stops as though it hit a rock an inch or two down, odds are that the ground is still frozen under the surface and you'll need to wait until soil temperatures warm up.

PLANTING USING THE NO-TILL METHOD

The no-till method of planting results in less soil disturbance but it requires adequate soil structure in the garden. Adequate soil structure is achievable by managing existing soil using the techniques described in this chapter. If your soil is healthy enough for no-till planting, you should be able to slide your trowel or shovel into the soil easily, move aside enough soil to accommodate the rootball being planted, then quickly move excess soil back around the plant's rootball to ensure good root-to-soil contact. Benefits of no-till include less erosion potential, less disruption of natural soil ecosystem services, and less greenhouse gases emitted.

REDUCED-TILL PLANTING AT HOME

This is how you extrapolate the principle of zone tilling from agriculture into the home garden: leave the soil chunky. Remember, zone tillage is deep tillage in specific zones in the garden. Soil water infiltration happens better and faster in these designated areas.

When digging any planting hole, no matter how large the size, resist the urge to chop and smash soil chunks. This can be difficult, because we are all somehow ingrained with the need to break up soil particles to smaller and smaller pieces to make sure the soil is prepared for a new planting. The exact opposite is true. Leave the soil chunky when backfilling around a newly planted rootball. This helps the plant grow into surrounding soil more quickly: the soil retains much of its structure when soil peds are left intact and not demolished.

PROPER PLANTING TECHNIQUE

Follow this planting technique to limit soil disturbance and give plants the best start.

1. Choose the planting site and move any mulch on the surface to the side. Save it to reapply around the plant when finished planting. I like to move aside enough mulch so I have a bare spot to pile up soil dug out of the hole. This way, your soil is right next to the planting hole and doesn't make a mess in the garden bed. It also limits any buried weed seed from being dispersed at the soil surface.

2. Dig the hole just as deep and about 4 to 6 inches wider than the rootball being planted. Make sure you do not grind the soil structure down to powder. Leave it chunky.

3. Remove any large rocks or roots that pass through the planting hole. Mix the soil taken from the hole with a small amount of compost or worm castings. If using compost, mix it at about a 25 percent rate by volume. If using worm castings, use 2 tablespoons for small starter plants up to 1 cup for larger, more established plants. In my garden, I mulch with compost, so anytime I plant, I automatically get enough compost in the planting hole by default because it mixes into the soil.

4. Place the rootball in the planting hole, checking to make sure that its soil line is about an inch or two higher than the surrounding edge of the planting hole, because the rootball will settle over time.

5. Place the amended soil in the hole around the plant roots; avoid creating big air pockets around the roots. The soil pieces you're placing around the roots should be a variety of sizes, recreating soil structure at the planting site.

6. Continue adding soil until the soil line is level with the surrounding soil. When planting perennials or annuals, keep soil away from the center (or crown) of the plant, as this could smother it. When planting trees, shrubs, or other woody type plants, make sure you keep the trunk clear of soil to avoid damaging the plant.

7. Now that the plant is in the ground and its soil is restored to the same level as the surrounding soil, move any remaining soil to build up other areas of the garden.

8. Mulch around the new plant, using the mulch you set aside. The same rules apply: do not smother the plant with mulch or place mulch directly next to the stems or trunk.

9. Get ready to water. Add a dose of liquid soluble fertilizer (following package instructions) to the watering can, then add water. Use the force of the stream of water to mix up the liquid fertilizer so it disperses evenly in the water.

10. Give the plant several "drinks," watering a little at a time so the water has time to soak into the soil and doesn't spill away from your new plant. Make sure to water throughout the entire planting hole you dug initially so the disturbed soil gets saturated as well. This helps the newly planted soil restore contact with the surrounding, undisturbed soil.

△ Disturb the soil as little as possible when digging planting holes.

04

Organic Fertilizers and Amendments

Farmers apply millions of tons of fertilizer each year to grow the food that sustains us. Those plants and flowers you bought at your local garden center? They were spoon-fed fertilizer from the week they were born until they left the nursery. Fertilizers supply essential plant nutrients because, just like all forms of life on this planet, plants need nutrients to live and grow.

Plants obtain their nutrients from soil, air, and water, with most of the required nutrients absorbed through their roots in the soil profile. However, leaves take in carbon dioxide from the air and combine it with water to create sugars, the building blocks essential to plant growth. The oxygen we breathe is a byproduct of this reaction.

◁ Organic fertilizers feed the soil microbes so that they can support the plants.

△ Trees aren't just beautiful, they're carbon storage sinks!

This process occurs during photosynthesis inside plant leaf cells. The process of converting atmospheric carbon dioxide into sugars fixes carbon inside the plant, potentially resulting in long-term carbon storage. Long-lived plants store carbon in their roots, trunks, and branches.

In the vegetation cycle each growing season, carbon is built up in leaf biomass and then released back into the soil's carbon bank when the plants lose their leaves each fall. Both perennials and annual plants build and store carbon in their roots every growing season, and when these roots die back, they add those stored nutrients back to the soil nutrient bank as they are broken down by soil biology.

🌱 A MESSY GARDEN IS A HEALTHY GARDEN

Consider leaving ornamental gardens as-is at the end of the season to provide valuable winter habitat and potential food sources for beneficial insects. The wild look of a garden may not be for everyone, but this overwintering habitat can be an easy way to recruit these beneficial insects to take up residence in your garden.

Who Fertilizes the Forest?

Forests grow each year without any fertilizer inputs from us, so you might wonder why gardens don't grow the same way.

In the forest, organic matter is returned to the forest floor each year as leaves and branches fall to the ground and break down into soil. And forest soils have the advantage of being undisturbed soils, not moved about by human hands in any way. Naturally occurring nutrients are present in all soils, but in residential areas, construction topsoil is often mixed together with lower-quality subsoils, resulting in a compromised soil that requires soil amendments and fertilizer in order for plants to thrive.

Additionally, perennial and annual plants that grow in forests live and die back, but without human hands to remove these plant residues, they in turn break down and help feed the soil. Generally speaking, in our gardens we round up all fallen leaves each year and compost them or waste them by throwing them away.

Many gardeners clear out annual and perennial stems so the garden looks neat and tidy, not realizing that this removal process takes away organic matter that would have been broken down over time by microbial activities. When we remove the ability of nature to produce a supply of nutrients, we are required to fertilize plants in order for them to grow and thrive.

△ Forests naturally cycle nutrients as leaves and other plant materials fall, decompose, and are returned to the soil nutrient reservoir to once again be taken up by plants.

△ Cleaning up the garden removes debris that can potentially harbor pests and diseases, but being too tidy deprives the soil of natural sources of nutrients.

◁ Leave healthy annuals and perennials standing over the winter to provide food and cover for wildlife.

Nutrient Depletion Over Time

Fertilizing is especially important in areas such as the vegetable garden or in perennial gardens, such as cut-flower gardens. In these intensely managed gardens, plants use nutrients to grow, flower, and produce fruit and seeds, which are removed from the garden ecosystem when we harvest fruits and vegetables or remove that year's growth when we clean up at the end of the season. Anytime we remove plant growth—especially when removing vegetables from a veggie garden, because vegetables produce more biomass than most flowering annuals—we are removing nutrients from soil.

If we want to achieve similar production the following season or year, we need to replace the nutrients. Think of it as a piggy bank. If we remove funds from the piggy bank but don't replace the funds, the funds will gradually vanish.

One method of ensuring plenty of nutrients in soil is actually called *nutrient banking*. Banking nutrients means adding soil amendments and fertilizers that contain plant-essential nutrients to the garden so that the nutrients are available to plants year round during the growing season.

Great gardens start each year with a full soil "bank account" of necessary plant nutrients. If plant yields were down in your garden and you don't seem to be getting the growth you expect, odds are your nutrient bank is low and needs additions to bring it back up. Soil testing is crucial to understanding what nutrients are lacking and which may still be in the soil nutrient bank.

Fertilizer Basics

Quite simply, fertilizer is required to grow big, healthy plants and productive vegetables. To build up the soil nutrient bank, we must incorporate fertilizers and soil amendments into our gardens.

There are many different types of nutrients and plants require them in different amounts in order to grow well without limitation. The nutrients needed in large quantities are called *macronutrients*. Necessary plant macronutrients include nitrogen (N), phosphorus (P), potassium (K), calcium (Ca), magnesium (Mg), and sulfur (S).

The nutrients needed in small quantities are called *micronutrients*. Necessary micronutrients include iron (Fe), zinc (Zn), manganese (Mn), copper (Cu), molybdenum (Mo), and boron (B). General fertilizers provide many or all of these nutrients, while specific fertilizers are used to supply specific nutrients. Fertilizers can be organic (naturally occurring) or synthetic (manmade). Organic gardeners, of course, opt for using natural, organic fertilizers to supply nutrients to plants.

Plants require various nutrients to drive different aspects of their growth. Nitrogen, for example, is used to make amino acids and other building blocks; calcium is used to strengthen cell walls; and phosphorus is required to increase fruit size and seed set.

Good, nutrient-dense soil naturally produces beautiful plant growth.

NUTRIENT	FUNCTION OF SPECIFIC NUTRIENT IN PLANT CELLS
Boron	Cell wall formation, sugar transport, and metabolism
Calcium	Strengthens cell walls, helps improve plant health
Carbon	Component of organic compounds
Copper	Strengthens xylem, enzyme activator
Hydrogen	Driver of adenosine triphosphate (ATP) reaction to create glucose and oxygen during photosynthesis
Iron	Chlorophyll synthesis
Magnesium	Part of chlorophyll molecule, activates enzymes
Manganese	Aids in photosynthesis
Molybdnum	Aides in nitrogen synthesis, component of nitrogenase enzymes
Nitrogen	Used to synthesize proteins for plant growth, nucleic acids
Oxygen	Electron receptor during respiration (breaking down sugars)
Phosphorus	Essential for flower and fruit formation
Potassium	Involved in sugar transport, enzyme reactions, stomata control
Sulfur	Amino acid synthesis
Zinc	Auxin synthesis, helps pollen formation

Each nutrient has a specific functionality within a plant leaf, stem, root, fruit, or seed. If any particular nutrient becomes limited, the plant cannot resume healthy growth until the limited nutrient becomes available again. In some cases, plants can transport nutrients from lower leaves to upper new growth.

However, micronutrients cannot be transported from old growth to new growth easily, and can severely stunt plant growth if unavailable for plant root uptake. Part of diagnosing nutrient deficiencies in plants is observing where and how the symptoms show up, as some nutrients can move within plants while others do not.

How Long Do Plants Need to Be Fertilized?

As discussed earlier, because plant material is constantly being harvested from vegetable gardens rather than being returned to the soil, vegetable gardens are typically fertilized every year to keep the nutrient bank stocked.

In other types of gardens, any newly planted plant benefits from a fertilizer application to stimulate growth and establishment. For gardeners who grow showy, colorful flowers, the rule of thumb is that plants with large, dramatic flowers will typically require more fertilizing than other plants, particularly if those flowers are picked for vase arrangements rather than composted back into the soil. And finally, because container gardens are frequently (and heavily) watered, they will need more frequent feeding. A large hanging pot of ornamental flowers may well require a light feeding monthly during the growing season.

Eventually, ornamental plants such as trees, shrubs, and perennials will not require fertilizer additions to sustain plant growth. As plants increase in size, their roots extend farther and farther into the surrounding soil. The longer a plant is

△ Yellowing of lower leaves can indicate nitrogen or potassium deficiency.

Ready to Use

FERTIFEED
All Purpose Organic Plant Food

FertiFeed Ready To Use All-Purpose Plant Food
Net Weight 4lb. 12oz. (2.15kg)

GUARANTEED ANALYSIS

Total Nitrogen (N)..4%
      0.25% Ammoniacal Nitrogen
      0.25% Other Water Soluble Nitrogen
      3.5% Water Insoluble Nitrogen*
Available Phosphate (P205) 2%
Soluble Potash (K20) 2%
Calcium (Ca)..5%
Sulfur (S)..1%

Derived from aerobically composted turkey litter, feather meal, sulfate of potash, biochar, hydrated calcium aluminosilicate, and oyster flour. F1992

*3.5% slowly available nitrogen from aerobically composted turkey litter, feather meal, biochar, and hydrated sodium calcium aluminosilicate.

KEEP OUT OF REACH OF CHILDREN

---

alive, the more connected that plant is to the surrounding soil nutrient bank. If the plant leafs out in spring and leaves stay green throughout the growing season (no leaves turning yellow or looking strange otherwise), then odds are the tree's roots have connected into the soil nutrient bank and will not need supplemental fertilizer.

Vegetable gardens, though, will still require annual applications of compost to continue feeding soil microbes the organic matter they crave. If you notice a year of particularly poor growth, and irrigation is obviously not the culprit, it may be time to add fertilizer again. The only way to know for sure is to get the soil tested to see what nutrients are present and available in the soil and which are lacking.

Understanding Fertilizer Labels

Every fertilizer has a product label and on that label is every piece of information you need to know in order to use the fertilizer effectively, including the amounts of nutrients present and the application instructions. Every label has what's commonly referred to as the N-P-K numbers prominently displayed on the front of the package. Because nitrogen (N), phosphorus (P), and potassium (K) are the nutrients required in the largest quantity by plants, their presence in the soil is most important.

Flip over the label to the guaranteed analysis section to find a list of all the nutrients contained in the fertilizer, the quantity listed as a percentage, and from what substances the nutrients are derived.

The guaranteed analysis section is important if you are concerned about the sources of the nutrients. Vegans and vegetarians, for example, may want to avoid using fertilizers containing blood meal or bone meal. Look closely at the "derived from" statement to

◁ The guaranteed analysis numbers on a fertilizer label indicate the percentages of nitrogen, phosphorus, and potassium. Those numbers plus the instructions for application can help you calculate the amount of fertilizer to spread.

make sure these substances are not included in your fertilizer—sometimes they are only mentioned in the fine print.

Some fertilizers may contain sewage sludge, which is not allowed on certified organic farms. Other questionable fertilizer choices for the organic garden are ones made with synthetic chemical fertilizers.

Are Any Chemicals Allowed in Organic Gardens?

The answer to this question is trickier than you might think. Short answer: no, chemical use is not allowed if you want to call your garden a strictly organic one. But the long answer is more complicated, because there are some pesticides listed as approved for use on USDA Certified Organic farms, which implies they would be acceptable for any organic garden as well. Defining what is allowed and what is forbidden boils down to the distinction between natural and synthetic substances. In essence, most natural substances are allowed while synthetic substances are prohibited.

But to immediately complicate the issue, be aware that not everything that is natural is allowed on Certified Organic farms. There are many naturally occurring materials that are toxic to humans and other animals. Ground up-tobacco dust is one such example. It's natural, but cannot be used on Certified Organic farms as a means of pest control, due to its toxicity.

Certified Organic Farms

The USDA set up the National Organic Standards Board (NOSB) as a federal advisory committee to make recommendations to the USDA on rules and regulations for Certified Organic farms, including the important task of determining what substances should be allowed or prohibited. Its members are a group of public volunteers appointed by the Secretary of Agriculture. The USDA set up the National Organic Program (NOP) as an internal regulatory program to develop standards for organically certified farms.

The NOSB makes recommendations to the NOP. The NOP then sets standards related to production, monitors accreditation agents, and provides training for farms seeking USDA Organic Certification. The NOSB maintains the list of certified farms, monitors violations and complaints, and sets standards for international import or export of organic products. It is a lot more complicated than just stamping "APPROVED" on applications from farms that wish to become certified organic.

And just as some natural substances are not allowed, there are some synthetic materials that are approved for use on organic farms, provided they do not contribute to air, water, or soil contamination—with limits on how much and how often they can be used. Examples include disinfecting agents used on

▷ Organic farms are managed by a strict set of guidelines issued by the National Organic Standards Board.

▽ It takes time for a farm to be certified, which allows three years for previously used synthetic chemicals to degrade and exit the system.

irrigation equipment or for cleaning produce post-harvest. Copper sulfate is an example of a synthetic material with limited approval for use on Certified Organic farms.

While copper sulfate is synthetic, it is allowed for use as an algicide and fungicide, as long as the farmer follows the limitations on how much and often it is applied. There is also a stipulation that these synthetic substances shall be used only as a measure of last resort, and that less toxic, more natural remedies be applied first to control a pathogen outbreak. The NOSB maintains a list of these substances on public record.

If you want to get your farm recognized as Certified Organic by the USDA, the NOP is the best place to begin this process, as it provides free training on how to navigate the process. Some basic tenets include:

- No prohibited substances may be used on the property for three years prior to harvest. This allows time for any previously applied residual prohibited substances to degrade.

- All records must be kept for inputs on the farm. This allows certifying agents to review farm activities and confirm adherence to NOP regulations.

- Create an organic systems plan for the farm, which is part of the application submitted to the certifier. This plan documents your proposed farming activities, and confirms compliance with NOP regulations.

There are many consultants to employ in the creation of an organic systems plan, but the best friend to make in the process is your certifying agent. Find one by talking to your local organic certifier or by searching online for qualified organic certifying agents. She or he will be your best source of information to ensure a smooth application process.

GETTING CERTIFIED

While getting certified is a worthwhile endeavor, the process is designed for farms that want to sell crops to individuals and on the open market. If you are simply farming or gardening in your yard, as long as you are not selling to the general public, you can say your garden/farm is 100 percent organic. If you are selling more than $5,000 annually in farmed products, you may not use the term certified organic to describe your farm activities—unless you apply for and receive the USDA Certified Organic designation.

The certification is designed for the food supply chain, not for backyard growers, and not having certification does not stop the backyard grower from farming with organic methods. The real appeal of certification is in the right to use the USDA Organic Seal when marketing your products to consumers. The seal can only be used by USDA Certified Organic farms.

Mineral Use on Organic Farms

Minerals provide nutrients, but not all nutrients are minerals. "Mineral" refers to a substance that occurs in nature that can be mined and used as fertilizer. Examples of natural sources of minerals include rock phosphate, greensand, rock dust, Sul-Po-Mag, potassium sulfate, and various types of limestone.

Minerals are inorganic and are formed by natural geologic processes. Unlike organic materials, minerals were never alive, which gives them the designation of *inorganic*. Only materials that were technically once living can be classified as organic.

However, it's important to replenish lost mineral content when it has been lost due to soil erosion because minerals contain specific nutrients required by plants. Use a soil test to match mineral content of a soil amendment to needed nutrients when selecting minerals to amend the garden. Using a soil test result as a guide makes sure you're correcting soil nutrient deficits correctly and not adding too much of any one nutrient. Overusing any soil amendment, mineral or otherwise, can lead to nutrient eutrophication, which is when a body of water is over-rich in nutrients supplied by runoff. This causes problems with fish and wildlife downstream.

While regulations may change due to any number of factors, at the present time certain minerals, such as elemental sulfur, magnesium sulfate,

▽ Excess fertilizer runs into waterways, causing algae blooms. More fertilizer is not better!

and certain humic acids, are designated as allowed, but with restrictions. Certified Organic farms have to demonstrate that the soil is deficient in these elements in order to use them.

Other minerals are allowed for use without restriction. Designation depends on many factors taken into consideration by the NOSB when advising the NOP on substances that should be allowed or restricted.

Organic Fertilizers and Soil Amendments

Many nutrients can be supplied by minerals but, in an organic system, other required nutrients are provided by plant- or animal-based fertilizers. Commercially made organic fertilizers come in granular and liquid formulations. Granular, dry organic fertilizers are, in many cases, long-term sources of nutrients that require the work of microbes to become water soluble in the root zone and available to plants. Liquid fertilizers are immediately available to plants as they are already in a soluble form. Care must be taken to not over-apply either liquid or dry fertilizer, as this practice wastes money and risks contaminating local water sources.

MINERAL-BASED FERTILIZERS

Fertilizer	Nutrients provided
Azomite	Calcium, essential micronutrients
Copper sulfate	Copper, sulfur
Elemental sulfur	Sulfur
Greensand	Potassium, iron
Humic acid	Complex structure, provides nitrogen
Limestone	Calcium, magnesium
Magnesium sulfate	Magnesium, sulfur
Potassium sulfate	Potassium, sulfur
Rock phosphate	Phosphorus
Sul-Po-Mag	Sulfur, potassium, magnesium
Zeolite	Alumino-silicates, essential micronutrients

PLANT-BASED FERTILIZERS

Fertilizer	Nutrients provided
Alfalfa meal	Nitrogen, phosphorus, potassium
Cover crops	Nitrogen, calcium, potassium
Kelp meal	Nitrogen, essential micronutrients
Soybean meal	Nitrogen, phosphorus, potassium

ANIMAL-BASED FERTILIZERS

Fertilizer	Nutrients provided
Bone meal	Phosphorus, calcium
Crab meal	Calcium, nitrogen
Fish bone meal	Phosphorus, calcium
Fish emulsion	Phosphorus, calcium, nitrogen
Manure (cow, horse, chicken, rabbit, worm)	Nitrogen, essential nutrients

MINERAL AMENDMENTS

As mentioned previously, minerals for use in organic gardening include rock phosphate, greensand, rock dust, Sul-Po-Mag, potassium sulfate, limestone, and naturally occurring deposits, such as diatomaceous earth, Azomite, and zeolite. The table on page 63 lists most of the commercially available minerals and the nutrients they provide.

PLANT-BASED FERTILIZERS

There is a long list of commercially available fertilizers derived from plants, including everything from alfalfa meal to soybean meal. Most of these plant-based fertilizers are byproducts of another process. These byproducts, such as Neem cake and soybean meal, are repackaged and utilized because they have great fertilizer value. Others, such as alfalfa or kelp meal, are simply ground and processed as fertilizers.

For soybean meal to be approved for use on organic farms, the soybean meal supplier must prove and certify that the soybeans were non-GMO, because GMOs (Genetically Modified Organisms) are prohibited for use on USDA Certified Organic farms. (More discussion on GMO crops is in Chapter 8.) The table on page 63 shows most commercially available, plant-based fertilizers and the nutrients they provide.

ANIMAL-BASED FERTILIZERS

Many fertilizers are animal based. Most non-manure-type, animal-based fertilizers are the byproducts of raising animals for food. Some of these fertilizers include bloodmeal, bone meal, hoof and horn meal, feather meal, crab meal, fish bone meal, fish emulsion, and biosolids (a.k.a. sewage sludge).

Biosolids are prohibited for use in Certified Organic agriculture due to the presence of heavy metals, pharmaceuticals, and other substances that accumulate in this waste stream. While there are aspects of the conventional production of animals I may not agree with, I also believe that the byproducts of raising animals for food should be used as fertilizers to avoid losing these valuable nutrients to landfills. Using these valuable resources is a means of celebrating each animal's contribution to our worldwide requirements for food production.

△ Crab meal, alfalfa meal, Azomite, fish bone meal, kelp meal, zeolite, liquid fish emulsion, bone meal, soybean meal

△ Composted animal manures are nutrient-rich soil amendments.

△ Compost is the duct tape of the garden. It fixes nearly any problem: poor drainage, dense structure, low nutrient availability. It's always a good idea to add compost to a new garden bed.

With the finite availability of nutrients on the planet, we need to make the best use of everything we have available to us. The table on page 64 lists most commercially available animal-based fertilizers and the nutrients they provide.

Although there are people who disagree for moral reasons, animal manures can be used to make some of the best, high-nutrient composts. Cow, horse, chicken, rabbit, worm, or any other herbivore manure can be used, but never use pet waste from dogs, cats, or snakes—basically anything with a carnivore diet. Due to the high-protein diet carnivorous animals consume, these manures can carry diseases that affect humans and should be kept out of the garden and compost pile.

COMPOSTING

Compost is perhaps the most widely used soil amendment in the garden. In essence, composting is the process of capturing organic material and allowing it to break down into a form that is easily used by living plants for nutrients. Compost can be made from any organic materials, including leaves, straw, garden debris,

△ Piles of compost at commercial operations heat up to temperatures high enough to kill disease pathogens and weed seeds, plus quickly produce compost.

△ Passive composting is a good way for home gardeners to make their own compost.

kitchen/food waste, farm manures, and even human sewage sludge. Compost adds organic materials to the soil that increase water- and nutrient-holding capacity, as well as creating beneficial biology to enhance the root zone. Compost can be made either on a backyard scale or on a commercial scale—the materials and methods are the same—but the size and scope of operations are quite different.

To make compost, ingredients must be blended together in proper ratios and volumes to initiate the biological, chemical, and physical changes that must occur. This is not what occurs in many backyard "compost" piles, because many of us are simply too busy to process the materials with the weekly or biweekly turnings of the pile that allow for true composing decomposition to occur efficiently.

But there is nothing wrong with this passive composting method, as materials will rot and break down into compost-like materials over time. At least the materials are kept out of the landfill and the amount of energy expended to transport and process the materials that you compost is zero. Composting in the backyard also reduces the burden on future generations, as landfill space is always at a premium. The more organic materials we keep out of the landfill the better; plus, by composting in the backyard, we create our own free soil amendment.

How to Build a Compost Pile

If you have the time and inclination, it is possible to create true compost in the backyard, but special attention must be paid to the compost ingredients, process, and method. The necessary ingredients are "greens," which provide nitrogen, and "browns," which supply carbon to spur on the composting process, and they must be added in appropriate ratios.

Most composting sources recommend a 2 or 3 parts browns to 1 part greens by volume. Ingredients that provide carbon include leaves, straw, and/or shredded paper. Nitrogen is provided by kitchen scraps, grass clippings, and/or animal manures as recommended on page 64 in the animal-based fertilizer section. These materials should be layered in the compost pile, adding 2 to 3 parts carbon materials by volume after every single application of nitrogen materials. I like to gently press down the browns on top of the greens after adding them into the compost pile to ensure good contact of materials.

Properly made compost piles heat up entirely on their own, due to the presence of specific microbes in the compost pile. These organisms are already present in nature, and as soon as the pile is built with the right ratio of greens to browns, the biological process begins on its own, breaking down the organic materials and releasing heat and water as byproducts.

Compost thermometers can be used to monitor the internal temperature of the pile and the pile should be turned over completely when internal temperatures reach 130°F. Commercial compost operations strive to produce high-quality compost that must be turned at least five times, each time the pile achieves a temperature of 131°F. This ensures any weed seed and pathogens present in the pile are neutralized.

Even if you're not attempting to make commercial grade compost in your backyard, compost should be turned regularly to speed the process along. After a compost pile is built and begins steaming (if you're not monitoring temperature with a thermometer, steam is an indicator of a hot pile), you should start turning.

Turning should be more frequent at first while the microbes begin eating the organic matter. As the pile cools down, you can turn less frequently. There are compost gadgets for sale that claim to speed the process along, but nothing beats elbow grease and a good compost fork!

The composting process undergoes a set of changes driven by three major stages: *thermophilic* (hot, 110°F to 165°F) reactions, followed by *mesophilic* (moderate, approximately 80°F to 110°F) reactions, and then *cryophilic* (cold, below 80°F) reactions.

The stages are driven by different biological communities and the length of each stage is driven by the compost ingredients and methods used to process the compost. These biological communities are already present, but do not begin to actively grow and multiply unless conditions are perfect for them. When they use up the available food sources, the process starts to wane and the next stage begins. This proceeds until the cryophilic stage, when compost is curing at ambient or below-ambient temperatures.

△ Build a compost pile by layering green materials and brown materials over each other. Add chopped up dried leaves, grass clippings, kitchen scraps, and other matter layer by layer, keeping in mind that smaller pieces will decompose faster.

△ Use a pitchfork or garden fork to regularly turn the pile to mix the layers of materials, outside to center and center to outside. A healthy pile will gradually heat up as time passes.

△ Turning compost frequently introduces oxygen into the pile, which helps to speed the breakdown process.

△ Use a compost thermometer to keep tabs on the stages of decomposition within the pile.

🌱 IDENTIFYING COMPOST THAT IS READY FOR USE

You know the compost is done when it does not visually resemble any of its original ingredients, it is cool to the touch, and it smells like damp earth in springtime, with no unpleasant odor.

Here is a quick test to determine if your compost is done cooking. Place a couple cups of compost in a plastic bag. Seal the bag and place it in room temperature, away from direct sunlight. Open the bag up after seven days. Does the compost still smell earthy or does it smell rotten and horrible? If it smells good, it's likely ready to use in the garden. If it smells bad, it is not yet done cooking and curing.

If the compost is not done, turn the compost pile over and let it sit for another two weeks, then try the test again. Repeat until the bag opens up to reveal an earthy-smelling finished compost.

△ Compost makes a great vegetable garden mulch.

SELECTING A COMPOST BIN

I've described the ingredients and ratios used to create a compost pile; now let's select a type of bin. Compost bins can be elaborate, made from concrete blocks, or as simple as a bin made from wooden pallets nailed together or a simple piece of wire fencing looped in a circle. The most common compost bin available commercially is the plastic bin. The most basic compost "bin" is no bin at all—just a pile with no sides or structure surrounding it, but an actual container offers the advantage of corralling materials, controlling odors, and keeping animal pests from rummaging around in your compost pile.

MAINTAINING THE COMPOST PILE

Maintain your compost pile so it has roughly the same moisture content as a damp, wrung-out sponge: this is key to keeping the composting process going. If you squeeze your compost in your hand, you should only get a drop or two of water out. If you get a stream of water down your hand, the pile is too wet. But if you are not able to squeeze any moisture out, it is an indication that there's too little moisture present.

Another convenient diagnostic test: in the early stages, a compost heap that is unpleasantly smelly is usually one that is too wet. But if a young compost heap is not warm to the touch, it is likely too dry. Later, as the compost pile matures and is ready for use, it will no longer be warm to the touch.

Add moisture back into a dry compost pile by leaving the lid off when it's raining, or by watering it. In summer, I like to add my pasta water to the compost pile. It adds both needed moisture and feeds the compost with the carbohydrate sugars that dissolve off the pasta during the cooking process. Other gardeners may "seed" the compost pile with a handful of organic fertilizer.

USING COMPOST IN THE GARDEN

I recommend applying a 2-inch layer of compost to the vegetable garden twice per year, once in spring before planting spring or summer crops, and once in fall after the fall crops come out and you are putting the garden to bed for the winter. Adding compost in winter allows it to work into the soil by the time spring rolls around.

If only adding once per year, add the compost in spring for best results. If you don't have enough of your own compost for twice-yearly applications, though, it may be worth buying additional compost. Adding compost twice per year builds soil microbial numbers quickly and adds to beneficial organic matter levels in soil. Another way to build soil microbial numbers quickly is by brewing up some compost tea.

COMPOST TEA

For centuries, farmers and gardeners have been using a liquid concoction of organic material steeped in water to produce a highly nutritious "tea" for fertilizing plants. In recent days, compost tea has been heralded as a revolutionary way to brew up your own microbes to add to garden soil. Compost teas can be made in different ways. There are simple compost teas and complex compost teas. There are *aerobic* (oxygenated) compost teas as well as *anaerobic* (made without oxygen) compost teas. Some tea recipes call for additives to boost microbe growth.

My own experience with compost tea began with my grandmother in her garden at a very early age. Since the time when I was first tall enough to help in the garden, she allowed me to dunk the three-gallon bucket in a big 50-gallon trash

◁ Mark says hello to a cow at age 2 on his grandparents' farm in Illinois.

△ Compost tea is nature's liquid fertilizer.

can filled with some kind of magic potion, then take the water down the vegetable row to give each plant a good long drink.

I didn't realize until much later that she had collected "cow patties" from next door and put them into the 50-gallon trash can, then filled the trash can with water. She was creating an anaerobic manure tea. If she had used finished compost instead of cow excrement in the big trash can, she would have also been making anaerobic compost tea, because simply soaking any kind of composting material in water produces a classic anaerobic compost tea, which is sometimes called a compost extract. Whatever you call it, soaking compost or manure in water allows the nutrients to become soluble and available for plant or microbe uptake.

Although anaerobic teas are the classic formula, there are distinct advantages to oxygenating the compost tea as it steeps. By oxygenating, you breed a larger population of beneficial aerobic bacteria and fungi, and also reduce the smelly anaerobic bacteria.

APPLYING COMPOST TEAS TO THE GARDEN

Apply the diluted tea as a soil drench for all plants every three to four weeks. You can't over apply, but it's best not to waste it. Give each plant an equal amount, approximately equal to a regular watering. Once filtered, compost tea can also be applied as a foliar spray. Plants can take up water-soluble nutrient sprays through their leaves, and it also helps the leaf create a biological web of microbial growth on its surface. Soil drenching is my preferred application method, though, because it's easy and clean-up is a snap.

If using as a foliar spray, spray your plants at dawn for best results. This gives the microbes time to establish before the harsh UV light picks up later in the day. Some microbes can deploy defense mechanisms that help protect against premature oxidation by UV light—essentially making their own sunscreen to keep them from desiccating, or drying out. Cloudy days with no rain are ideal for foliar compost tea applications.

Always flush and clean all tanks, applicators, hoses, screens, and nozzles after every compost tea application. Otherwise your system will get all funky and gummed up with biofilms!

🌱 HOW TO BREW AEROBIC COMPOST TEA

If you want to brew up some tea at home, I suggest using aerobic brewing methods to reduce the potential for growing harmful bacteria such as E. coli. The most simple at-home brewer is constructed from materials readily found at pet stores and hardware stores. You'll need a five-gallon bucket, 15 feet of aquarium tubing, a small air pump (get one made for a 10-gallon tank), two air stones, and a few connectors.

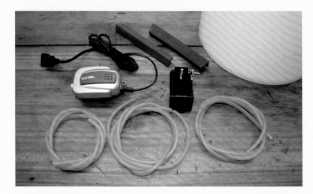

1. Gather these basic materials required to run a compost tea setup at home.

2. Connect the air pump with your air stones using the aquarium tubing.

4. Make sure the tubing is long enough so that the air stones sit at the bottom of the bucket. The air pump should remain in a safe place outside the bucket so it does not get wet.

3. Split the tubing coming off the air pump using a Y connector, so you end up with two lines. Attach both air stones to these lines, one air stone per line.

5. Fill the five-gallon bucket with four gallons of water. You need to leave the extra space to accommodate the bubbling that will ensue once brewing begins.

(continued)

6. Drop in the air stones and begin bubbling the water for about 30 minutes before going to the next step. (For those with city water this is a required step to remove any chlorine present. If you have rural well water, you can skip this step.) After about 30 minutes the chlorine will evaporate, and you can add your compost. Keep the air pump going the whole time. The water temperature has a big impact on how fast the brewing process starts. Warmer water encourages more microbial activity; microbial cellular reactions practically double for every gain in 18°F (10°C). The microbial activity in the compost tea will actually raise the tea temperature.

7. Prepare the compost by placing it inside a single-layer cheesecloth or burlap bundle tied up to keep large particles from going into the solution. If you don't mind filtering your compost tea later, you can add compost directly to the bubbling water. Whether or not you filter depends on application method in the garden. To keep it from clogging your watering can or irrigation system, use a filter layer of cheesecloth or burlap to strain out the compost when you pour the liquid into a watering can.

8. Brew the compost tea for 24 hours in a place that can easily be cleaned up. After about 12 hours, the tea will start to bubble quite a bit, and may even bubble up over the top of the bucket. This is especially true if you are adding supplemental sources of nutrients to encourage specific groups of microbes. Supplemental nutrient sources such as molasses feed bacteria and those such as fish emulsion feed fungi. If using on a lawn, you want your tea to be dominated by bacteria. If you are using it on trees only, you want your tea to be dominated by fungi. If using in vegetable or ornamental gardens, you want a tea that is balanced with amounts of active bacteria and active fungi.

After 24 hours, your tea will be ready to use. Keep the air stones going until all the tea is removed from the brewer. This ensures that your tea stays aerobic until you apply it. Place the compost tea in your water can, blending it with 100-percent dechlorinated water. If using city water, remember to let it sit long enough to allow the chlorine to evaporate before combining with your brewed tea. If you don't take the time to get rid of the chlorine, you will kill off many of the microbes you just brewed. For best results, pre-bubble tap water by placing air stones into the water at least four hours in advance and have it ready for this step, or use rain-barrel water.

Making Your Own Growth Enhancers

If you weren't yet convinced that plants are amazing, here is another reason why plants are one of the greatest resources we have on this planet: You can use plants to make compounds that help other plants grow. Plants produce growth-promoting substances in small quantities in their cells and transport them to areas in the organism where they are needed. You can use this to your own ends to provide natural growth enhancers in your garden. This kind of solution represents the epitome of organic gardening practice—using byproducts of plants themselves to stimulate plant growth.

Examples of these plant growth-promoting substances include *gibberellins*, *auxins*, and *cytokinins*. These substances are plant hormones that are produced naturally during times of need to fulfill specific plant functions. Kelp—a form of seaweed—is a favored source of these compounds often used by gardeners to give their plants a boost. The microbial metabolites present in worm castings are another source of these vital plant hormones. Make sure to read product labels to determine the source material if you go shopping for amendments that provide these substances promoting plant growth. Many off-the-shelf products contain synthetic versions of these naturally occurring hormones.

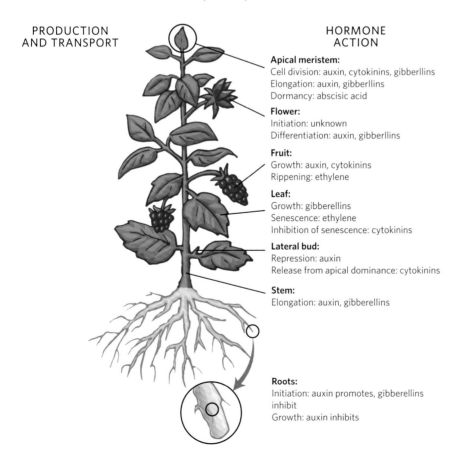

GIBBERELLIN, AUXIN, AND CYTOKININ

PRODUCTION AND TRANSPORT

HORMONE ACTION

Apical meristem:
Cell division: auxin, cytokinins, gibberllins
Elongation: auxin, gibberllins
Dormancy: abscisic acid

Flower:
Initiation: unknown
Differentiation: auxin, gibberllins

Fruit:
Growth: auxin, cytokinins
Rippening: ethylene

Leaf:
Growth: gibberellins
Senescence: ethylene
Inhibition of senescence: cytokinins

Lateral bud:
Repression: auxin
Release from apical dominance: cytokinins

Stem:
Elongation: auxin, gibberellins

Roots:
Initiation: auxin promotes, gibberellins inhibit
Growth: auxin inhibits

▷ It's easy to make your own fertilizer from comfrey.

Did you know you can make your own fertilizer at home? One such example involves taking the leaves and stems of comfrey plants (*Symphytum officinale*) and soaking them in a tub of water. A seven-day soak is enough for the leaves to leach their fertilizer contents into their bath water. Give the liquid a stir or agitate about once per day to help things along, then use the entire batch on the seventh day. Dilute your comfrey tea 1:1 with water, and use as a soil drench.

Another great source of nutrients is something we all produce every day. Urine contains a lot of nitrogen and other nutrients, but is so strong it must be diluted approximately 20:1 with water to make sure you don't burn your plants. Excess amounts of nitrogen can produce a salt burn that causes root dieback when applied as a soil drench. Diluting this powerful fertilizer provides nutrient levels that roots can handle.

If you can handle this method of generating fertilizer in your garden, place straw bales in the garden in strategic places and "water" them with urine. The nitrogen absorbed by the urine helps break down the straw and makes it a great soil amendment to add to the compost pile or used as mulch. Another way to capture this resource is to place a bucket with *biochar* in a hidden corner of the garden where you can "water" it with urine. Biochar is a wonderful adsorbent (see page 78), and the nutrients present in the urine will help charge up the biochar.

△ Raw biochar

△ Compost blended with biochar

Biochar: A Supercharger for Soil Productivity

Biochar is an ancient technology more than 2,000 years old, with roots in the Amazon. The native people of the Amazon basin created charcoal and mixed it into their soil. These skilled farmers must have experimented with methods to enhance their soil and paid attention to the resulting harvests, or perhaps they stumbled upon the results by watching nature take its course after a forest fire. Regardless of how they discovered it, these indigenous people unlocked soil productivity by making biochar and incorporating it into their agricultural soils.

To this day, the soils of the Amazon region are known as *terra preta*, or black earth, and are known for their productivity. Even 2,000 years later, crops can be grown in this soil with little to no additional fertilizer application. Comparing native soils of the region to the modified biochar-enhanced soils, it becomes obvious how much more fertile the biochar-enhanced soils are. The terra preta soils are dark black as far as three feet deep, while the native soils are reddish. Terra preta soils enhance plant growth and yield so much that the locals sell the soil itself as a beneficial soil amendment for non-terra preta soils.

Biochar is essential carbon that is used in amending soil. It is created by burning organic materials in the absence of oxygen, a process known as *pyrolysis*. This produces a highly porous carbon that improves nutrient *adsorption* and provides a nearly permanent home for beneficial soil biology. When added to soil, it produces a highly porous structure that holds water and nutrients until times of drought, at which point plant roots can access the stored water contained in the micropores of biochar particles.

▷ The perfect time to apply a pre-inoculated biochar to the soil is during new garden construction. Follow the directions on the biochar label you purchase, but shoot for 5 percent of biochar in the soil by volume.

Biochar improves nutrient adsorption. Nutrients are adsorbed on clay particulates and organic matter due to the high cation exchange capacity (CEC) of the clays and organic matter. Adsorption means nutrients are held by the clays or organic matter. Think of it as holding onto another person's hand. You become adsorbed to each other. In the case of nutrients in soil, it is the chemical charge of one material that hangs onto another. Absorption is the process of absorbing one thing into another. You absorb food every time you sit down to eat. Roots absorb nutrients from the surrounding soil. Nutrients are held in soil by adsorption. That, my friends, is the difference between adsorption and absorption.

Biochar is a growth and yield booster because its pure carbon structure retains nutrients and acts as a high-rise apartment for soil microbes. Due to its high CEC, it is an incredible garden tool that makes soil more fertile by increasing its nutrient-holding capacity. Before biochar can start releasing nutrients back to plants, however, it needs to be inoculated and charged up. Once charged, the resultant biochar blend is ready to use on all types of plants.

There are many ways of charging biochar. Think of raw biochar as an empty battery that needs to be charged before it can function. If considering charging raw biochar, do lots of research and decide for yourself what nutrients you want to use to charge the biochar. Then mix said ingredients with some beneficial biology, such as compost and/or worm castings. Biochar is often also charged with a carbon source, such as flour, for microbes to consume as food. It is up to the individual to decide what inoculation process and materials fit into their personal organic paradigm.

High-quality biochar has a high carbon and low ash content, giving it a slightly alkaline pH. Once blended into your potting soil or garden soil, it will not significantly change soil pH but it will improve plant growth and yield. Good biochar is highly porous, which results in an incredibly high surface area. More surface area means more sites for nutrient-holding capacity and more surface area for beneficial soil microbes to live and thrive.

HOW BIOCHAR IS MADE

Biochar is made by burning organic materials in an enclosed system in the absence of oxygen, a process known as pyrolysis. These systems range from small table-top versions to industrial units that can heat entire warehouses or greenhouses. The smallest size unit is called a or top-lit updraft (TLUD) stove. These small units are perfect for short-term use. TLUDs were originally designed for use in developing countries where food is cooked over an open flame inside the home, causing a smoke hazard. TLUD stoves offer a cleaner method of cooking with the side benefit of creating small amounts of biochar with each batch.

If you're looking for a novel way to produce small amounts of biochar at home, a TLUD stove could be just the ticket for you. Each batch makes about 1 to 2 cups of finished biochar. You will know the batch is done when the flames coming out of the TLUD change from larger red, orange, and yellow flames to a smaller, consistently blue flame.

Once the flames start to shrink back into the unit, without any bursts of yellow flames, the pyrolysis process is complete and the biochar inside the unit can be dumped out to drench and cool. Always use caution when attempting to make biochar, as coals can reignite unless sufficiently cooled and saturated with water. Always wear protective equipment. Safety first!

However, if you want to produce larger amounts of biochar, you'll need to look for a larger unit. Google "Biochar with two-barrel nested retort." You'll get links to all kinds of YouTube videos with people making biochar in large metal drums.

The process is quite simple once you get set up. You must have a 50-gallon drum for the outside and a 30-gallon drum for the inside. Both drums need lids. The 30-gallon lid stays intact, but the 50-gallon lid needs a hole on top where a chimney can be placed. This helps create air draw through the unit.

There are many design variations on the double-barrel retort (DBR), but this is the basic plan:

Drill ¾-inch holes in the 30-gallon and 50-gallon drums to allow flammable gases to move from the 30-gallon drum into the 50-gallon drum. The holes should be approximately 6 inches from the base of each drum, all the way around the drum, spaced about 6 inches apart. The gas exchange feeds the fire in the outer drum but starves the inner drum of oxygen.

Fill the 30-gallon drum with dry materials such as wood chips, scrap wood, or bamboo, or sticks and branches from the garden. Center the 30-gallon drum inside the 50-gallon drum, then loosely pack flammable materials around the outside of the 30-gallon drum and light them.

△ Biochar-making setup

When the fire coming out of the bottom of the outer drum changes to mostly blue flames, the flammable materials inside the inner drum have been burned off. The remaining material is biochar: pure carbon.

WHY USE BIOCHAR?

Mixing biochar into the soil adds carbon to the soil profile. Because it is practically a permanent soil amendment (especially in terms of a human lifetime), these carbon additions are a good way to store carbon in the soil. In this way, biochar can help in the fight against climate change by sequestering carbon in the ground. It helps sandy, well-drained soils hold moisture, and when added to clay-dominated soils with poor drainage, biochar helps increase air space. This increase in porosity and air space helps slow the conversion of soil nitrogen to gaseous forms that are lost to the atmosphere.

BIOCHAR APPLICATIONS FOR THE GARDEN

Biochar must be inoculated, or charged, before being applied to garden beds. If incorporated in a raw state, plant growth will suffer the first year as the biochar pulls nutrients from the surrounding soil to charge itself. Biochar is like a battery: it has to be charged up before it can work.

A simple recipe for application is a 50/50 blend of biochar and compost. More advanced blends incorporate additional sources of microbes and nutrients to charge the biochar. Look for raw biochar and ready-to-apply biochar blend at your local garden center if you don't want to make it yourself. When applying to soil garden beds, spread a biochar blend in a ½-inch layer and mix into the top 5 inches of soil. One cubic foot of a biochar blend will cover approximately 24 square feet of area. If growing in containers, combine 1 cubic foot of a biochar blend containing 50 percent biochar with 9 cubic feet of your preferred growing media, whether it's potting soil or 100 percent coconut coir fiber. Mix well, and plant away.

A beautiful thing about biochar is its recalcitrance in soil. Recalcitrant materials break down slowly over time—remarkably slowly in some cases. The carbon structure created during the pyrolysis process is incredibly stable. The terra preta soils of the Amazon have been carbon-dated to 2,000 years ago. While it's hard to fathom organic material surviving that long in soil, it still remains to this day. In terms of a human lifetime, adding the appropriate amount of biochar one time to your garden beds will result in a lifetime amendment.

Cover Crops

Cover crops are sown to literally cover the soil with plant growth. We plant them to help deter soil erosion, protect soil structure, suppress weeds, build soil nitrogen reserves, and build soil organic matter. While cover crops can be used year-round, most cover crops are sown in late fall to provide winter cover. Some cover crops are killed by winter's cold, while some tough out the harsh conditions and need to be tilled under in spring to kill the plants and add nutrients back into the soil.

Choose a cover crop—or blend of cover crops—based on where you garden, how soon your first frost comes, and what your intentions are. Some cover crops, such as forage radish, are great at breaking up compacted soil and drawing nutrients up from the subsoil. Other cover crops, such as peas, vetch, or clover, are great at fixing nitrogen from the atmosphere into the soil. Some cover crops, including wheat or rye, are grown specifically to add organic matter and cover the soil surface to prevent erosion or changes in soil structure. Cover crops such as buckwheat are chosen for good performance during the summer season.

COVER CROP TYPE	PROS	CONS
Buckwheat	Fast grower, heat tolerant, improves soil aggregation	Requires well-drained soil, flooding will rot plants
Field peas	Good nitrogen fixation, combine with oats	Susceptible to root rot
Hairy vetch	Excellent nitrogen fixation, weed suppression, winter hardy	Slow to establish
Oats	Fast grower, good nurse crop for other plants	Not winter hardy, shallow rooting
Rye	Tolerates cool growing conditions and heavy clay	Can suppress other plants
White clover	Nitrogen-fixing perennial, tolerates high-traffic areas	Carrier for legume diseases
Winter wheat	Winter hardy, provides harvestable grain, helps prevent root rot in vegetables	Must wait 2 to 3 weeks before planting next crop to avoid nitrogen tie-up

△ Cover crops are most often sown in the fall.

◁ While traditionally used on large farm fields, cover crops offer the same benefits to smaller gardens.

Mulch

What's the big deal about mulch? The simple reason to love mulch is that using it reduces the workload of the organic gardener. Mulching the garden helps conserve soil moisture, suppresses weeds, and protects against infection by plant pathogens. Mulch protects plant leaves from getting splashed by rain drops that hit bare soil, which can land microscopic fungal spores, bacteria, or other microbes onto leaf and/or fruit surfaces and spread plant pathogens. Your local garden center or bulk landscape supplier are the best go-to places when shopping for mulch.

WHEN TO APPLY MULCH

The best time to mulch in spring is after soil temperatures have begun to rise, but before the soil begins to dry out. That leaves a fairly narrow window for the optimal application time. Soil temperatures can be measured by a soil thermometer or you can get the general idea by paying attention to how quickly turf grass begins to green up and grow in springtime. Once turf grass starts growing, you can generally be sure that the soil has warmed enough to apply mulch; however, if mulch is applied too early, soil warming is slowed, which in turn slows plant growth.

In the Mid-Atlantic, where I live, most spring mulch applications go down around April 1. Make sure to get the mulch down before your perennials start coming up, so you don't destroy the tender, emerging foliage. Most plants can push through a thin layer of mulch, but you want to avoid smashing tender new growth with a wayward shovel of mulch.

△ Mulch to keep the garden tidy, conserve moisture, add organic matter to the soil, and suppress weeds. Leave a small bare ring around plant stems when applying mulch to prevent plants from rotting.

BEST MULCH TYPES

While technically anything covering the ground is considered a mulch, mulches can generally be divided into fine or coarse. Shredded bark, compost, or pine fines are good examples of fine mulch, while wood chips, pine nuggets, or straw are good examples of coarse mulch. Choose a type the fits your landscape aesthetic and intended purpose. Materials such as straw or pine fines with a low C:N ratio are best in vegetable gardens. Longer-lasting materials such as wood chips have a higher C:N ratio and are best for pathways to protect soil from compaction by foot traffic.

Organic gardeners should choose natural, undyed mulches for their gardens. Dyed mulches are known for keeping their color, but the coloration chemicals can leach into your soil or sidewalks. Some companies will grind up old pallets, construction debris, or other scrap wood and dye it to the standard black, brown,

△ A properly mulched tree.

△ Coarse mulch is most often used in landscape beds.

or red. These materials take longer to break down because they have not been subjected to composting and may contain contaminants.

Avoiding dyed products isn't hard, because there are plenty of good natural options when it comes to mulch. If you're looking for black mulch, there's nothing better than 100 percent compost. If you're going for brown mulch, use pine fines. If you like the reddish look, try pine needles (also known as pine straw). For all these natural options, make sure it's coming from a high-quality, commercially produced source so you're not adding any weed seeds or plant pathogens.

HOW MUCH TO MULCH

Fine mulches should be applied at a depth of no more than two inches. Coarse mulches require thicker applications of up to six inches to achieve weed suppression and moisture retention. But please avoid the mulch volcano: heaping up cones of mulch around the trunks of trees. It is frequently done around newly planted trees but it is a disastrous practice, as it increases the chance of the tree getting infected by pathogens. Mulch placed against a tree trunk holds extra moisture, which is an invitation to soil fungi to grow on the tree trunk. If left in place for years, the tree will decline from the base due to fungal rot.

To avoid this, keep at least a three-inch mulch-free zone around the base of trees. Mulch should be applied from this point to just beyond the tree drip line. The drip line is a term used to demarcate the soil area covered by the tree canopy. Mulch should extend just beyond the tree canopy for best results. Do not pile mulch around annual, perennial, or vegetable stems, either, because this, too, can create favorable conditions for pathogens.

FREQUENCY OF APPLICATION

Apply mulch seasonally to maintain a two-inch layer if using fine mulches or up to a six-inch layer if using coarse mulches. Some people pay to have landscaping companies remove old mulch and replace it with fresh each year. While the urge to maintain a fresh look is understandable, removing old mulch really isn't necessary from a garden health point of view. As long as the existing mulch layer is raked over to break up any matting, it can remain in garden beds. Fresh mulch can be added on top.

Do not till woody mulches directly into soil. As wood breaks down, it takes nitrogen from the soil, which means less nitrogen is available for uptake by plant roots. If you need to till a mulched area, remove the mulch first and set it aside. Then, reapply the mulch once the garden project is done in that area. Only mulches that are fully aged, composted, or those with a low C:N ratio can be tilled directly into the garden.

Choose Wisely

Choosing fertilizers for your organic garden is largely a matter of personal preference, but your choice should be tempered by science. Your decisions are guided by soil test results and specific fertilizers are selected based on their ability to provide necessary nutrients and how these fertilizers mesh with your outlook on life. Vegans and vegetarians concerned with animal welfare are able to select fertilizers that mesh with their values by avoiding products with animal-based ingredients. Omnivores can pick fertilizers that best suit their soil needs, while still choosing to avoid certain fertilizers.

Compost, compost tea, biochar, cover crops, and mulch all have a role to play to maintain soil health in the garden. How many of these tools you use depends on personal preferences and level of investment in the garden. Incorporating all these tools will improve the productivity and decrease the workload in your organic garden.

△ Apply a finer mulch in vegetable gardens. It will break down over time and add nutrients to the soil.

△ Just say "no" to mulch volcanoes! Mounding mulch up against a plant stem creates a moist habitat for bacteria, fungi, insects, and small mammals to thrive and damage the tree trunk.

05

Water-Smart Organic Gardening

Water is a precious resource in the world—perhaps the most precious of all, next to air—so organic gardeners in particular are intensely interested in not wasting it. Only three percent of the water covering the Earth is freshwater (that is, not saltwater), and of that, much is tied up in underground sources and glaciers. In the United States, the biggest consumers of water are turf fields (including lawns) and commercial agriculture, but everything we do at home and in the garden impacts our freshwater supplies, locally and globally.

As organic gardeners, we want to always be conscious of our water use. Never leave the hose running down the driveway while you're off doing something else. Install a breaker valve so you can turn off the hose end when needed.

◁ Rain barrels are a handy source of water for container gardens.

Plants are between 60 and 90 percent water by mass, meaning that water management in the garden is crucial for a big vegetable harvest or beautiful landscape. In organic gardening, look at all water available on your property, including tap-, well-, and rainwater, and carefully consider the best way to use it to benefit your plants. Efficiency is key to water management in organic gardens.

Starting with Soil

A repeating theme for organic gardeners and for this book is that everything starts with the soil. The soil is, essentially, the repository for everything a plant needs in order to grow, except for the carbon dioxide provided by the atmosphere. The structure and composition of soil determine water absorption and retention rates, which, when combined with natural rainfall amounts, determine when and how much you'll need to water plants.

If your soil is coarse and low in organic matter, chances are good that you'll have to water more frequently because the soil will drain quickly. To increase water-holding capacity in soil, you can regularly add compost. Fine-textured soils high in organic matter drain slowly. Chapter 3 discusses soil structure, cautioning against overworking the soil, not only because it disrupts living organisms in the soil, but because it can also wreck its structure and decrease water-holding and draining capacity.

More water is not necessarily better and it is as easy to kill a plant from over-watering as it is by under-watering. The trick is delivering the right amount of water for the plants you're growing and the soil you're growing them in.

Water Sources

Before jumping into the ins and outs of various water sources, it's important to note that the chemical properties of water can influence the soil and thus the plants growing in it. If your plants are exhibiting symptoms of nutrient deficiencies, the water could have something to do with the problem. Usually this is related to soil pH and many gardeners simply amend the soil to lower or raise the pH. But that's not always enough if the pH problems are stemming from the water source.

In addition to testing your soil, test the pH of your water supply, using an inexpensive pool testing kit. Municipal water often has a high (alkaline) pH, which can limit plant nutrient uptake. This creates a problem for ornamental plants, such as azaleas and hydrangeas, and for many edible crops that grow better in slightly acidic to neutral conditions. (There are exceptions: brassica vegetables, such as broccoli, cauliflower, kale, mustard, and radish, are examples; they grow just fine in slightly alkaline, higher-pH soils.)

If your water source is alkaline (approximately pH 8 or higher), try using liquid fertilizers such as fish emulsion, which are slightly acidic. That can balance out the

UNDERSTANDING THE WATER CYCLE AND GROUNDWATER

Freshwater supplies across the Earth are found in two different forms. Surface water refers to the water that is visible in some form—freshwater lakes, reservoirs, and streams or glaciers and snow-pack held frozen in mountainous regions. When these water supplies dwindle, it is visually obvious, such as the crisis situations noted in recent years when major reservoir reserves dropped dramatically, or when glaciers recede.

Much of the freshwater used for human needs is not surface water at all, but instead is found in underground lakes or rivers or bound up in porous sands or soils hundreds or thousands of feet underground. This water is known as *groundwater* and it is in many ways the more important source of freshwater—and the most difficult to preserve due to its invisible nature.

Ecologically, the Earth is a closed system, so no water leaves or enters the system. As global warming melts glaciers, for example, that water causes sea levels to rise. There is no net loss of water on the planet. However, water does move around through the system and it is not always redistributed to the same areas from which it is being removed. A prime example of this is the American West, where groundwater is being removed much faster than it can be replenished.

Much of the water used for daily living comes from groundwater, so efforts to conserve and replenish it are important for organic gardeners. Water conservation methods apply to all of us, no matter where we live.

In elementary school, we all learned the basic water cycle:

• Precipitation moves water from the air—as rain or snow—to the ground. Ideally, water percolates into the ground to replenish sources of groundwater or to be taken up by growing plants.

But much of the precipitating water flows through storm water systems and into streams, rivers, and lakes, eventually making its way to oceans, where the alkalinity renders it unusable to humans until . . .

• . . . water moves back into the air in the form of vapor through evaporation or transpiration. Water evaporated from the vast oceans enters the atmosphere, where it once again can fall as freshwater precipitation and seep down to replenish groundwater supplies. Additional water returns to the atmosphere as plants transpire water through their leaves as a byproduct of respiration. Eventually, this water vapor will again condense into precipitation.

This is a never-ending cycle, but moving groundwater up from the depths of the Earth into municipal, agricultural, or landscape systems changes the natural flow of water. In developed areas where the population exceeds the natural capacity to replace groundwater supplies, drought problems occur.

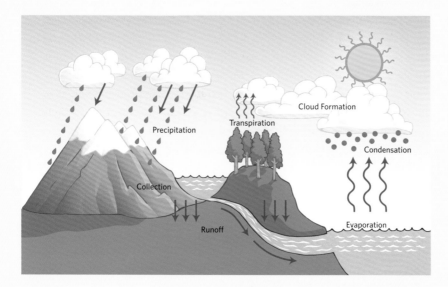

◁ The Earth is a closed system and all water supplies are finite. Plants take up water, which is then transpired through their leaves. Water evaporates into the air, condenses, and forms clouds. Precipitation replaces surface and groundwater supplies, and the system repeats in perpetuity.

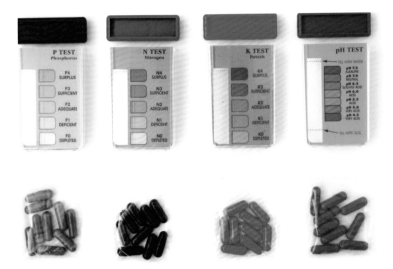

▷ If you notice nutrient deficiencies in your plants and you've already done a soil test, the next step is to test the water, as the pH could be off.

pH and make fertilizer more readily available to plant roots. A quick trick to get water pH down if you're using it to water houseplants is to drop one water-soluble tablet of aspirin per gallon in your watering can. Give it an hour or so to dissolve, give it a quick stir, then water. The salicylic acid released by the aspirin will slightly lower the pH of the water.

RAINWATER

Rainwater is a tremendous source of water for gardeners in many areas of the country—one that largely goes untapped. Instead, rainwater hits roofs, pavement, and impervious surfaces and runs off into storm drains, or, in the case of smart, progressive gardeners or building managers, into rain gardens or onsite treatment areas. There's no reason not to harvest rainwater for gardening use. It's simple to install rain barrels and cisterns, though be aware that in some parts of the country, rainwater is viewed as a community resource and there may be restrictions on your rights to harvest rainwater. Rainwater quality depends somewhat on the air quality where you live but while is not potable (safe for drinking without treatment), it is fine for the garden.

Harvesting the rainwater that runs off your roof can provide you with enough supplemental water for container gardens and, in some cases, small vegetable gardens. You can buy rain barrel kits, make your own rain barrel to catch water, or use a larger cistern. A standard seven-gallon rain barrel fills up quickly during a rainstorm, so if you're serious about harvesting rainwater, install a larger rain barrel or cistern at each downspout and consider putting multiple barrels together to increase storage capacity.

Rain barrels usually sit on stands between 12 to 36 inches in height. Gravity provides enough water pressure so that a spigot placed low on the barrel can be used. If you are catching rainwater in larger cisterns, it may require a pump to distribute the collected water.

△ To harvest more rainwater, connect rain barrels together. There are many ways to configure a system, depending on the type of rain barrels you have.

◁ Rain barrels are easy to install. See instructions on the next page.

1. Build a platform to raise your rain barrels up off the ground. This height will allow gravity to assist in providing pressure for water flow. The best location is near an existing roof downspout.

2. The rain barrels will need to be close together in order to link the barrels with tubing that will allow the others to fill after the first barrel becomes full. Some rain barrels have nipples designed to connect the barrels; when one fills, the overflow then begins to fill the other.

2. Variation: Hose kits are available that allow barrels to be joined together if they have no overflow nipples.

3. Attach outlet hoses to the outlet nipple on the barrels. In the simplest form of this system, you can simply use the hoses to empty the barrels one at a time.

3. Variation: You can also tie your rain barrel outlet hoses together with a Y fitting so that they funnel through one hose. This will increase the water pressure, as the downward force of two or more barrels will be pressuring the hose at the same time.

4. In this installation, the homeowner has created an impromptu "spigot" fed by both rain barrels to conveniently fill watering containers. It is important that the spigot be below the level of the outlet openings on the rain barrels in order for the barrels to empty fully.

5. Arrange the downspout so it will dump water into one of the connected rain barrels. Make sure the tops of the rain barrels are fitted with screens so that debris and insect larvae cannot fall into them. Without protective screens, rain barrels can become breeding grounds for mosquitoes.

MUNICIPAL WATER

If you live in the city or a large incorporated area, you probably receive your water from a municipal water supply. Depending on the supply, restrictions, and costs, watering from this source is often the most convenient and best option—after your rain barrels are empty, of course.

Municipal water is always treated, usually with chlorine and fluoride. Depending on how the water is treated, other chemicals may also be used. Municipal water almost always has a pH above neutral, which as previously mentioned can cause problems with plants and require additional attention to the soil. If you are watering with municipal water, it is important to test the water for pH and other chemicals, and to treat the water, if necessary, to make it more ideal for plants. Depending on water quality, it can be very expensive to treat your own water. A simple solution to high-pH water is to drop a tablet of water-soluble aspirin into a gallon of water. Salicylic acid is a metabolite of aspirin and will help lower the pH of water after dissolving in it.

WELL WATER

Even if your main water source is municipal water, you can still install a well to use for watering your plants. Usually, well water is exempt from municipal water restrictions put in place during droughts. If you live in a rural or unincorporated area, your entire water system is likely to source from a well. As is true of harvesting rainwater, though, some regions may have restrictions on if you can drill your own well, to what depth and how much water you can pull from groundwater supplies. In regions where groundwater supplies are in crisis, always consult with your local authorities before drilling your own well.

Wells pump groundwater up to the surface where it can be used for plants and people. The composition of well water, including pH and types of minerals dissolved in the water, vary from location to location. These elements can cause problems with interior plumbing, but are unlikely to cause problems with plants. Still, if a nutrient deficiency is showing up in your plants, it is worth testing the water to see if it could be the issue.

GREYWATER

Greywater is the water from sinks, laundry machines, showers, and bathtubs. While not potable, it is still relatively clean and can be filtered and recycled for use in the landscape. There are local and national regulations as to how greywater should be recycled and for what purposes it can be used. If you're gung-ho to recycle water from your home, you can have a home system installed. This might or might not be practical for your budget. Check with local contractors and municipalities for guidelines on installing a greywater reuse system for your home.

Even without a dedicated greywater system, it is possible to save and recycle water from around the house. Again, you have to decide whether it is practical for your lifestyle. Water from boiling vegetables and pasta, unused water in drinking glasses, and water that runs while you wait for the shower to warm up can all be captured and used in the garden or to water houseplants. Water is heavy, though, so if you're serious about saving shower or bath water, you might want a barrel mounted on wheels.

Watering Systems

There are two main ways to water the garden: manually or with an automatic irrigation system. Both have pros and cons, so you'll have to decide which will work best for your garden and your lifestyle.

MANUAL WATERING

Any watering method that's not set semi-permanently in place can be classified as manual watering. A watering can, a hose, a sprinkler that you drag around, and watering with a breaker attached to the end of a watering wand or hose are manual methods. A breaker is a type of hose-end attachment that breaks up the strong stream of water that comes out of a hose.

△ My ultimate tools for hand watering—a breaker and watering wand with brass shut-off valve—allow me to precisely control the direction and flow of water.

Manual watering options are great for small-space gardens where you might not be able to separate plants with different watering needs as you can in a larger area. Manual methods also work well for newly planted trees and shrubs that need extra TLC for a month or two after planting but that will be left to their own devices once established. Basically, manual watering methods are appropriate for any space where watering needs are variable within a small area or narrow window of time. Manual watering is less efficient, both in terms of time and water usage, than micro irrigation that automatic systems can afford, but it has its uses. If you're collecting water in a rain barrel, you'll likely distribute via a watering can, although with a larger cistern system, it is possible to hook up a hose and pump. If you do this, though, just make sure not to suck the barrel dry and burn out the pump. Once you empty a cistern, unplug or turn off the pump to keep it in good working condition.

Tools for manual watering:

- Hose
- Sprinkler
- Breaker
- Watering can
- Wand
- Rain barrel
- Shut-off valve

For manual watering, it makes sense to spend enough money to get a nice hose, shut-off valve, watering wand, and water breaker. If you take care of them and don't leave them outside during the winter, they will last for years and will help you conserve water.

HYBRID SOLUTIONS

Hybrid watering solutions are closer to manual systems than to automatic irrigation, but they do offer some flexibility and buy some time so that you don't have to run out with a hose every day or multiple times a day.

Self-watering containers, or very large containers, are a must if you're growing vegetables in container gardens during the summer. Fill up a self-watering container reservoir a couple of times per week and your plants will have a consistent moisture source, which will help you avoid cultural problems, such as blossom end rot on tomatoes or peppers.

Gator bags are excellent for newly planted trees, giving them constant moisture during the critical time of root establishment.

Some types of irrigation, such as one-piece soaker hoses, are more flexible for moving around than others, such as micro irrigation systems that include multiple pieces. Within landscapes, it's common to have full underground irrigation systems installed, though I would encourage you to cultivate ornamental landscapes that are well suited to your environment and natural rainfall, and that do not require extra water.

△ Self-watering containers are great for frequent travelers or gardeners in areas with hot summers. Such containers eliminate problems caused by repeated wet/dry cycles.

INSTALLING A SOAKER HOSE

Soaker hoses are great for small vegetable gardens, raised beds, and gardens near a water source. These hoses are made of a porous material that allows water to slowly seep into the ground surrounding them, but be aware that water pressure and the amount of water distributed will decrease the farther you get from the water source. Soaker hoses work best in flat areas, and unlike manual watering methods and spray-type irrigation heads, they automatically deliver water directly to the soil, keeping it off plant leaves and decreasing the spread of fungal infections.

Caution: Do not turn the faucet all the way on when running a soaker hose. These hoses require much less water pressure than a typical faucet is capable of putting out. It will take some trial and error to regulate this perfectly. If the hose is leaking water readily but no water is spraying out onto nearby plants, it's perfect.

To install the soaker hose, follow these steps:

1. Connect the hose to the water source, starting with the backflow preventer, then the timer, pressure regulator, a length of garden hose to reach the beginning of the soaker hose, and finally the soaker hose itself.

2. Wind the soaker hose around the plant rows, leaving at least 2 inches between the plant stems and the hose. (If the hose is stiff, leave it out in the sun and it will be easier to bend and maneuver.) The hose does not need to run next to every plant, but the spacing should be arranged so that the soil is evenly moist. Fast-draining soils will require more hose to accomplish this than slow-draining soils.

3. Top with mulch to keep the hose from drying out and to keep it lying flat. This also helps prevent the sun from damaging the hose.

INSTALLING A MICRO IRRIGATION SYSTEM

Micro irrigation, sometimes referred to as drip irrigation, allows for the most efficient use of water, but it is the most expensive and time-consuming system to set up. It will, if well cared for, last a long time. Soaker hoses are a good micro irrigation "cheat" if you don't want to buy and set up an entire system. The main reason to use drip or micro irrigation is that it delivers water directly to the root system, which conserves water and prevents the spread of disease.

You can buy micro irrigation kits that come with all the pieces you need, or you can assemble your own system. Some systems are designed with emitter hoses (which are like soaker hoses, but with defined, drilled holes at controlled intervals) or drip tape; while other systems have emitter tubes or spaghetti tubes that run off a central distribution line.

The constant with all micro irrigation systems is that they require a pressurized water source to push water to the various emitters. You'll install a backflow preventer (required by most municipalities) and a pressure regulator to ensure the proper water pressure within the system. Without enough pressure, the water won't travel through the tubes and emit properly; but too much water pressure can cause leaks and blowouts within the system.

△ Soaker hoses are effective, simple drip irrigation options.

◁ Micro irrigation systems allow you to evenly deliver water right to the plant root systems.

Typical components of micro irrigation systems:

- Water source
- Backflow prevention device
- Timer
- Filter
- Pressure control valve
- Emitters
- Distribution lines to move water through the system
- Valves to control water movement through the system
- Connectors for hooking different lengths of tubing together

If you purchase a kit it will come with an instruction manual with tips for installation. Here is the general installation sequence:

1. Connect the backflow preventer, timer, filter, and pressure valve to the water source, in that order.

2. Connect the drip hose or distribution hose to the water source, at the end of the pressure valve.

3. Run the hose around plants in the landscape or construct a distribution network within vegetable gardens, using various valves, corners, and connectors.

4. When the hoses and distribution tubes are where you want them, use a punch to create holes for inserting emitters near the plants.

5. Turn on the system and test it.

The following are handy micro irrigation tips.

- Plant first and then lay tubing around shrubs, perennials, and annuals. This way you cut each piece of tubing the perfect length for each plant.

- If installing new irrigation in a vegetable garden, plan for frequently used spacing. For example, you might have one set of spacing for tomatoes, peppers, and eggplants, and a different measurement for greens. Once you punch holes in the tubes, they're set for the life of the tube. You can move the tubes to accommodate crop rotation, but you can't change where the holes are. (This will force you to be a bit more regular with vegetable garden design and spacing.)

- Follow directions for row and tube/tape spacing. You need to make sure there is adequate water coverage at the plants' root zones. If you run the system and the water is not reaching the plant roots, move the hoses.

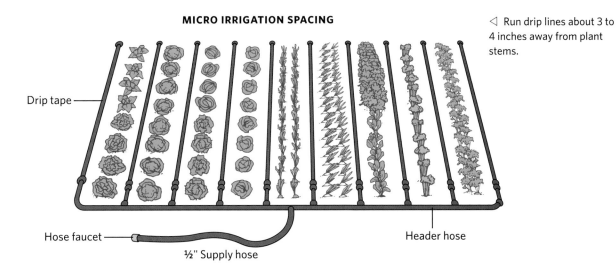

MICRO IRRIGATION SPACING

◁ Run drip lines about 3 to 4 inches away from plant stems.

Drip tape

Hose faucet

½" Supply hose

Header hose

When and How Much to Water

Watering plants doesn't happen on a regular schedule. Plants need water when they need water and their needs changes based on time of year, climate, and soil type. Irrigation systems can be constructed with timers, but that is for convenience (so you don't have to stand outside with a hose for hours), accuracy (to know how much water plants are receiving), and for vacations/travel. You can't set a timer and forget about it all summer, but instead must monitor the soil conditions regularly. Soil type impacts frequency of watering, as do the types of plants you're growing and the length of time they've been established. Soils high in clay and/or organic matter retain water for longer than soils that are sandy, rocky, and/or low in organic matter.

Most plants start to slightly curl or shrivel when they need water. Some take on a grayish cast. You'll know the lawn needs to be watered, for example, when it looks more gray than green or when grass depressed by footfalls doesn't immediately spring back up.

Always water newly planted plants immediately after planting them. This is the most crucial watering they will receive in their lives. This first watering establishes capillary action in the surrounding soil around the plants, and connects plant roots to the water matrix in the broader soil area.

Capillary action is the phenomenon by which water molecules are attracted to each other and drawn upward within a soil column. In coarse soils, water molecules stick together in larger clumps, making them heavier and harder to pull up and quicker to drain down. Fine-textured soils have smaller pores, resulting in smaller water clumps and slower movement.

Watering at the time of planting establishes capillary action and ensures a constant supply of moisture to plant roots, as long as there is moisture available in

CAPILLARY ACTION

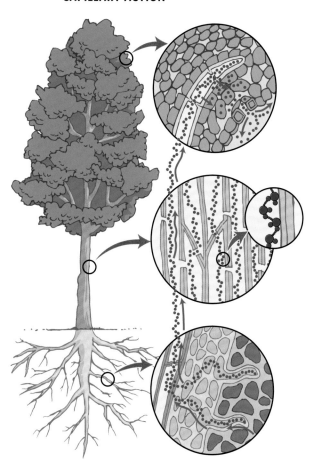

△ Capillary action is a combination of cohesion, adhesion, and surface tension between water molecules and the environment around them. It creates the continuous column of water running from the soil, through the plant roots, up through the plant, and finally from plant leaves to the air. It is part of what allows plants to stand upright.

the soil. You're actually helping to establish one long continuous column of water from the soil up through the top of the plants. Transpiration (part of the water cycle) is the process of water being pulled up from the roots of the plant, used for internal plant functioning, and finally passed out through the plant's leaves.

On hot and windy days, plants can transpire more water than they can take up through the roots, which results in wilting. That's important to note when deciding whether to water your plants. Just because the plants look wilted doesn't mean they need water. If the soil feels moist, the problem is that the plants can't move water quickly enough to maintain good pressure. This is typical of hot summer afternoons. Always check the soil for moisture before running for a hose or watering can. Sometimes the plants will perk up as soon as evening falls or direct sunlight passes.

Whenever you water, think "deep and infrequent." Watering newly planted plants deeply a few days per week as opposed to shallowly every day encourages the plants to grow deep roots, which improves their drought tolerance.

As your gardening experience grows, you'll learn how to recognize when plants need water. Here are some guidelines for different types of plants.

Newly planted trees and shrubs, including edibles.
Water newly planted trees and shrubs thoroughly at the time of planting. Hold the hose and water breaker at the base of the tree, on the wide open setting, for about a minute. Make sure to move the hose around the plant, so water is distributed evenly and doesn't run away from the plant. Then close the breaker slightly, leaving the hose to drip, or leave a soaker hose around the tree for an hour or two, longer for larger plants, especially on fine-textured soils.

Water twice weekly with a slow-drip irrigation for an hour or so. Keep this schedule through the first growing season. If you have a tree, you can use a gator bag or similar device to function as the slow-drip irrigation.

△ Plants will sometimes wilt or roll up their leaves to minimize water loss on hot, windy days, regardless of moisture availability in the soil.

◁ Using gator bags is an easy way to water new trees.

Established landscape trees and shrubs. I do not regularly water ornamental trees and shrubs in the landscape once they've been in the ground for a year. Either they make it or they don't. One key way to be a responsible organic gardener is to choose plants that are well-suited to their living conditions. If you live in an area with low rainfall, don't plant trees and shrubs with high water requirements.

If you live in an area that sees frequent rain and you're experiencing a rare drought (no water for a month or more), give trees and shrubs planted less than two years prior a deep soak every couple of weeks. That's it. Just enough to keep them from dying.

Established fruit trees and shrubs. Fruit trees and shrubs need more water than ornamentals because you're asking them to do something for you—produce an edible harvest. In times of drought, provide 1 to 3 gallons of water per fruit tree or shrub per week—more for larger plants. You'll have a better harvest.

Newly planted annuals, perennials, and vegetables. These types of plants are the fussiest, and use the most water when first planted. The best way to know if you need to water these is to check the soil. When first planted, the soil around annuals, perennials, and vegetables should be about as damp as a wrung-out sponge, and it should stay that way as the plants are establishing roots. This could mean watering every day in southern climates or coarse-textured soils. In temperate climates, water every other day as new plants establish, or every few days if it is cooler when you plant. Don't drown your plants! Check the soil for moisture and keep it at the same moisture level as a wrung-out sponge.

Succulents. Succulents have more water reserves contained within their leaves than other plants. They will also rot much faster than other plant types when overwatered. Water newly planted succulents once, and then wait until the soil dries out to water again. This is the general rule with succulents, newly planted or not.

Established annuals and vegetables. Annuals and vegetables tend to need more water than woody trees and shrubs or perennials. They're smaller and have smaller reserves. With edibles in particular, fluctuating water availability leads to cultural problems, such as blossom end rot or a smaller harvest. Water evenly to ensure that the soil is consistently about as moist as a wrung-out sponge. Soaker hoses are lifesavers for vegetable gardens.

Established perennials. I don't water established perennials unless there's a massive drought requiring me to water trees and shrubs. If you want to grow water-loving perennials, create a small pond and grow pond-margin perennials around the edge. Living by this rule really requires that you are gardening with perennials well adapted to your environment. A southwest garden with northern

△ Succulents are low-water plants but they are not no-water plants.

woodland perennials, for example, will have trouble following my rule. But a genuine organic gardener will gradually adapt his or her garden so it makes efficient use of water.

Bulbs. Water bulbs at the time of planting so that they can establish roots. After that, the bulbs should not need extra water. Too much water will cause them to rot, and definitely do not water spring-blooming bulbs during the summer. Summer bloomers, including Asiatic lilies, can be watered every couple of weeks if you're not receiving regular rain. Most garden species planted from bulbs or tubers originate from dry regions, such as the Mediterranean or Mexico, and so require minimal watering.

Lawns. See Chapter 11 for lawn care information.

Timing of Watering

Whenever possible, water plants early in the morning. This allows any water that might land on the leaves to dry before evening. Fungal and bacterial diseases spread through water, so the sooner any surface water dries from the plants, the lower the chance for disease to spread. Soaker hoses are my preferred method for watering, not just because they're less work once installed but because they deliver water directly to the soil, lessening the chance of disease spread.

In small spaces where soaker hoses are not practical, my number one tool is the watering wand with breaker attached to the hose with a shut-off valve. Always use the shut-off valve when you move between pots or beds so that you don't waste water.

Effects of Overwatering and Under-Watering

Plants in the landscape are more likely to die from under-watering than over-watering, especially right after planting. Immediately after planting, roots haven't yet grown into surrounding soil and therefore are unlikely to be flooded with water.

Plants in containers, though, can suffer from both overwatering and under-watering; overwatering is common immediately after plants are planted. Once the soil in a container is saturated, the only way for the soil to dry out is for plants to use the water or for the water to slowly evaporate from the soil surface.

Frequent under-watering can result in "permanent wilting point." This is a point at which the soil moisture is so low that it causes a total collapse of the water pressure from root to leaf; it is a turning point from which plants cannot recover. In containers, this tends to happen later in the summer between waterings. It's why I advocate for self-watering containers or really big containers for edibles and recommend that your potting soil contains worm castings and compost. As long as the reservoir is full in a self-watering container, the plants won't run out of water. Similarly, worm castings or compost will hold moisture and prevent the soil from drying out completely between waterings.

For landscape plants, problems stemming from under-watering are usually more pronounced at the time of planting. It's why watering thoroughly at the time of planting is so important in order to establish the capillary action immediately. If the capillary cycle is broken, watering the soil is the only thing that re-establishes it. The larger the plants get, the bigger and deeper the root system grows, resulting in more root hairs on the roots to soak up water and maintain water pressure within the plant, but immediately after being transplanted, plants have few root hairs to draw in the water.

Resist the urge to water every time you see a plant wilting. It is always a good idea to check the soil. If it isn't dry throughout the top inch of soil, there's enough water available for plants. In this case, the wilting is likely simply because the plants are transpiring water faster than they can take it up. If you water when there is available water in the soil, you risk causing problems by overwatering.

It is possible for the soil to be too wet—in containers or in the landscape. Like any living thing, plants can be drowned if inundated with too much water. The oxygen that plants require for respiration comes from the soil and if the soil is completely saturated, they're unable to take up that oxygen.

△ Self-watering containers standardize soil moisture, making it easier to grow plants such as tomatoes without problems with blossom end rot.

Water Wisely

Fresh water is a precious resource. Collect and reuse it when possible, and never waste it. Resist the urge to water every time you see a plant wilting. Check the soil for moisture before watering. If it isn't dry in the top inch, don't water.

Newly planted plants need more frequent irrigation compared to established plants. Water early in the day to reduce evaporative loss and lessen disease pressure. In the end, choose the watering methods that work best for you. As long as you're not wasting water, you'll be a long way toward embracing organic gardening principles.

06

Care, Cultivation, and Conditions

Now that we've discussed fertilization and water needs as they apply to organic gardening practice, we turn to the remaining cultural considerations: sun exposure, wind prevalence, soil moisture levels, mature plant size, and physical environmental conditions, all of which have a part to play in organic gardening. Providing proper care and culture goes a long way toward avoiding the common problems with pests and diseases that could discourage your devotion to the organic gardening path.

Perhaps you are planning a new garden—if you've purchased a new home, for example, or have signed up for a community garden plot for the first time. Or maybe after some time as a gardener, you've decided to start fresh with a new approach or a new layout. Whatever the reason, spending some time planning the cultivation of your next garden pays off in the long run.

◁ The best way to have a gorgeous garden? Give it the right care!

Assessing Cultural Conditions

This is the most important place to start because it will ensure that you follow the mantra, "Right plant, right place." You can't know if you're planting the right plant in the right place unless you know what your "place" offers and how that compares to what the plants need.

Nicola Ferguson wrote *Right Plant, Right Place* in 1984 and it has been a mantra for many landscape designers and gardeners ever since. Placing a plant in the right conditions does more to help that plant grow and thrive than almost any other variable. If the plant requires full sun for best results and you plant it in shade, for example, the plant will putter along, growing slowly and sporadically, and may divert from its predictable form, showing reduced flowering and/or leaf size. The same is true if you stick a plant that prefers shade into full sun.

Many gardeners have the experience of having rather poor specimens suddenly thrive when they are transplanted into a different location, sometimes only a few feet from their original location. Or, more mysteriously, plants will sometimes take it upon themselves to migrate, moving themselves over a period of several growing seasons until they find an ideal spot to thrive.

Soil type is also an important factor when making plant choices. Due to site conditions and slope, soils may be perennially dry or wet. There are plenty of plants that do well in either condition, but you must consider this when planting. Placing a plant that prefers dry roots in a spot that is perennially wet during winter is a sure-fire way to kill that plant, even if it is hardy in your zone. Research plant requirements to determine if the plant you want will handle the soil conditions in your garden. There are many lists out there, such as plants for dry shade, plants for wet soil in full sun, and so on. When in doubt, head to your local garden center. Tell them the soil and sun conditions you have and the intended garden use or function and they will guide you in the right direction, providing options that are suited to the garden conditions in question.

When plants are not grown in ideal conditions, it makes them more susceptible to insect infestations. Under less than ideal conditions, plants have reduced leaf coverage, which can snowball into other problems based on plant physiology. Fewer leaves offers less ability to create energy for the plant, which leads to less root growth, which creates a reduced ability to uptake water and nutrients from soil. This domino effect can be avoided simply by planting in the right place from the start.

Healthy plants have a variety of mechanisms to defend against insects. Some plants can increase the presence of bitter-tasting compounds in their leaves to deter insects from feeding on them. Other plants have been shown to produce salicylic acid (the same active ingredient in aspirin) to ward off insect damage. Healthy plants are better able to defend against insect attacks, even if that defense is simply to grow out fresh foliage and stay ahead of the insect.

Another reason to make sure you're planting in the right place is to reduce the need for pesticide use in the garden. Remember, there are organic pesticides that gardeners and farmers can use to control pests and diseases. However, very healthy plants will require nearly no pesticide application at all to maintain their "curb appeal." When I worked as a plant heath care specialist, I saw the right plant, right place rule broken over and over again, as plants succumbed to insects after being planted in locations that offered non-ideal conditions. Educating yourself is the best way to overcome this expensive form of maintenance.

So, before you pick out plants for your garden, take a stroll and make notes of the conditions in areas you plan to garden. Here's what to evaluate.

SUNLIGHT

The amount of sun or shade will help determine the best plant options for a given area. Spend some time truly thinking about and observing the site. Watch the sun track across the sky in summer and again in winter. This shows you the path the sun takes throughout the year, and indicates which areas of your garden have more sun than others.

Look at the space you're working on. Does it receive morning sun immediately after the sun comes up? How long does it get full sun before it starts to get shaded later in the day? Does it get afternoon sun? If so, how much? Does it get shade all day? Are there trees shading the garden space or are buildings casting the shade? Measure in hours for making the easiest comparisons. You may be surprised, for example, to realize that an overall sunny garden area has a spot or two that gets shade most of the day—spots where shade-loving specimen plants can happily thrive. Or, you may find that a narrow swath of ground between two houses actually gets a fair amount of sun and could be a prime spot for a short row of tomatoes or another vegetable.

Once you've documented the amount of sunlight in your garden spaces, you can plot out garden areas using a priority system. If you only have a little area with full sun and you want a vegetable garden, the choice is a quick and easy one: the full sun area is where you need to put that vegetable garden. If you don't have an area with at least 8 hours of sun, don't fret, as you can still grow veggies in less than 8 hours of full sun per day. In fact, some leafy greens and herbs prefer 4 hours of sun per day.

Experiment. If certain plants do not bear much fruit, try other crops. You're guaranteed to find some that will do well for you no matter how much or how little sun your garden receives. You can always convert the space to another use if the veggie garden doesn't produce well for you. When designing your garden, start with the highest priority garden elements—the garden spaces you want the most. Over time, you can tackle the remaining garden areas and decide what you'd like to develop.

WIND

Is the garden space you're considering subject to harsh winds? Maybe the space never sees a breeze due to the placement of evergreen windbreaks. Wind can offer

△ Shade garden

△ Sun garden

When shopping for plants at a garden center, check out the plant tags, as they're designed with the gardener in mind and should provide a lot of information about the plant, including sunlight requirements. Typically, they will use terms such as *full sun*, *part sun/part shade,* or *shade.* Sometimes this will be indicated with a symbol—a small full sun or a sun half obscured, indicating part shade, for example.

If a tag lists the plant's requirements as *full sun*, it is generally saying the plant does best with at least 8 hours of full sun. If a tag says *part sun*, it is generally saying the plant will do well with at least 4 hours of sun per day. (*Part sun* is really the same thing as *part shade*.) *Full shade* would be areas that

receive about 8 hours of shade per day. Not all shade is created equal, however. Shade cast by buildings is darker than shade cast by tree branches. Trees can create what is called dappled shade, which means some sunlight streams through the branches throughout the day but plants will remain mostly shaded by tree branches and leaves during the growing season. And a site that is densely shaded during mid-summer may well be much sunnier in early spring before the trees have leafed out. A great place for sun-loving spring bulbs can be a spot that eventually will see deep summer shade once the tree canopies are fleshed out.

a cooling breeze in summer but it also affects how cold or warm a garden is in winter. Plants do not feel a wind chill like we do; in fact, a slight breeze on frosty nights can help keep cold air from settling around tender plants, actually making them "warmer." At temperatures far below 32°F, breezes have less impact on a plant's cold hardiness; however, wind can still dry out leaves and branches in winter. Cold air is generally drier than warm air and harsh winter wind can dry out foliage by removing precious moisture from leaves and stems, especially on evergreen (conifer) trees and shrubs. Some tender plants may benefit from wrapping in burlap and/or mulching with leaves.

HARDINESS ZONE

The geography of the United States is categorized by a system of numbered USDA hardiness zones based on average winter low temperature. Higher zone numbers indicate warmer daily temperatures during winter months; lower zone numbers indicate colder average temperatures in winter. Every plant has an ideal zone range for peak growth and hardiness (surviving the winter). Choose landscape and ornamental plants that do best in your zone for lower-maintenance gardening. A plant's hardiness zone will be listed on the plant tag or plant description. If you're up to the challenge, you can create a microclimate to protect what would otherwise be a tender plant in your zone. Annuals are not considered "hardy" plants, as they are replanted each year.

Cheating a plant's zone recommendation by placing it in a spot where there is a lot of winter sun does not work. In fact, it is much the opposite. What kills a plant is really the frost/thaw cycle during winter. A plant with a borderline zone rating that is subject to sudden momentary thaws because it gets direct sun in midwinter will very likely die, but if it is in a more sheltered location where it does not thaw then refreeze constantly, it may survive nicely. For example, if you want to grow zone 5 plants in your zone 4 garden, the best place is out of the direct winter sun.

Buildings can also help create a microclimate because south-facing walls absorb heat from the winter sun and radiate it back out at night. Even a couple degree difference can be enough to protect a plant that is one hardiness zone up from yours.

❧ DRESSING PLANTS IN WINTER COATS

In my Zone 6B garden, we protect our figs by wrapping them with burlap and filling the burlap "coat" with leaves. Use zip ties or similar fasteners to secure the burlap wrap on itself, but do not tie zip ties onto the tree branches themselves. When I visited gardens in Minnesota, I saw burlap bags full of leaves placed on the soil around tree trunks like a blanket to protect their roots in winter. Although a landscape with evergreen shrubs shrouded in faded burlap might not be the most aesthetically pleasing sight, if you are intent on growing a particular tree or shrub, cloaking them with burlap in winter might make the difference between death and survival.

Another Minnesota gardener has managed to keep a Japanese maple—which rarely survives outdoors in the upper Midwest—alive and thriving for several years by heaping a large mound of snow shoveled off the sidewalk over the trunk and lower branches of the tree during the winter to insulate it from the bitter cold and thaw-freeze cycles.

WATER

Some plants require more water than others to thrive in the garden. Grouping plants with similar watering requirements is another example of "right plant, right place" gardening. If you plant lavender next to a tomato plant, the lavender will suffer, as it does not require as much water as a tomato plant. For healthy gardens, group dry-soil-loving plants together and moisture-loving plants together in soil that meets their needs. This doesn't mean you won't ever have to water plants, but planting a succulent in a bog garden is a recipe for sudden plant death.

Organic also involves making the best plant choices for your region. Choose drought-tolerant plants if you are gardening in a dry climate because plant choices that require tremendous amounts of water to survive in dry climates are not naturally sustainable. An organic gardener, for example, would find the massive expanses of green, non-native turfgrass lawns in the desert southwest United States as a rather shameful waste of valuable resources. The organic gardener quickly learns that regionally appropriate plants can provide just as much beauty with a fraction of the water use.

SOIL TYPE

Most plants are fairly adaptable and will thrive in good garden soil—soil with good structure, a fairly neutral to slightly acidic pH, adequate moisture, and good drainage. There are some exceptions, such as ericaceous plants (blueberries, azaleas, and hollies) that need acidic soil; or succulents, which need sharply draining soil. All of your work determining the type and qualities of your soil comes into play now. Make sure to review and make notes about soil type for your eventual plant shopping trip.

MICROCLIMATES AND SPECIAL CONDITIONS

Specific conditions that influence plant selection include atmospheric pollution in urban gardens, where certain plant species are better able to withstand pollution generated by vehicle traffic. Use common sense when choosing plants for urban gardens. Planting edible plants curbside may not be the best choice, as they will inevitably be coated by particulate exhaust emitted by passing vehicles or by road salts spread over streets to treat ice. Along the coast, certain plants do better when subjected to daily winds blowing in salty ocean air than others. To avoid disappointment, do a bit of research beforehand to determine a plant list that is appropriate for all site conditions present in your garden.

△ Bricks, pathways, sidewalks, walls, and hardscape absorb heat, block wind, and create a microclimate that's generally warmer than surrounding areas.

△ Don't plant trees under or close to power lines.

AVAILABLE SPACE

How large is the space where you're planning to plant? Will the space accommodate what you're planning to put there? When shopping and siting a plant, research and consider its eventual mature size. At the nursery or garden center, plant tags are a valuable source of this information. Do not plant trees that will grow to 30 feet wide and 60 feet tall under power lines or near buildings. Give big trees the room they need to grow into their mature form. If size is an issue, choose smaller trees or shrubs that fill the space without being a problem.

When planted in the wrong place, plants require constant pruning to stay within the confines of the design space. This pruning results in an unnatural shape and subjects the plant to constant open wounds, which can be an entry point for insects or diseases. Look for plants bred for compact spaces if your garden is best described as "cozy."

SURROUNDING INFRASTRUCTURE

When choosing plants, take into account the surrounding infrastructure. Some plants, such as maple trees, are shallow rooted and should not be placed next to sidewalks or driveways. Their roots grow under these structures over time and as the plant increases in size, so do the plant roots. Eventually, plant roots will crack and heave sidewalks and driveways, leading to expensive repairs.

Plants can also damage water lines. Roots grow where they find water. If pipes on the property, including irrigation lines, leak at all, you can be guaranteed plant roots will seek out this source of moisture. Roots will grow into pipes and crack them apart even more while searching for water. If left long enough, roots can eventually block the water flow in pipes entirely.

Trees are the biggest culprits when it comes to this issue. Choose shallow-rooted plants when planting near incoming water lines, septic fields, or irrigation hubs. Smaller plants, such as annuals, bulbs, and perennials, are good choices for these areas. Remember you may have to dig up these areas at some point if you have a problem, and smaller plants are easier to relocate. Always check with your local municipality before digging deeply in your garden. Most communities—or the utilities companies themselves—have a service that will visit your property and identify water mains or power and gas lines that run through your property.

Selecting Plants

Now that you know which conditions your garden offers to prospective plants you can go shopping! In addition to selecting plants that will grow well in the cultural conditions your garden offers, you also want to make sure you're purchasing the healthiest plants available.

ABOVE THE SOIL LINE

Look for plants that look lush, healthy, and full. There should be no obvious insect problems, discolored leaves, or evidence of leaf drop. Look for trees that have been pruned properly to establish good structure. The plant should not have moldy, squishy, or rotten parts. The aboveground portion of the plant speaks volumes about the root system below the surface of the soil. If the top of a plant looks unhealthy but no insects are present, odds are it's suffering from some problem in the root zone. Below ground is where plants take in all their nutrients and water, so a well-developed root system is key to root health.

△ When shopping for plants, it can be tempting to hit the bargain shelf. When possible, buy healthy plants that look green and robust: they're worth the higher price.

△ A girdling root can wrap around a tree trunk, cutting off circulation of water and sugars underneath the bark, which effectively strangles the tree.

BELOW GROUND

Usually a plant that looks healthy on top will have healthy roots as well, but there could be another story going on below the surface and the health of the root system should be accounted for when choosing plants.

Plants are traditionally grown in round black plastic pots. Only recently have other types of containers started to appear on the market, including fiber containers that help increase air space in the root zone and encourage root branching. It pays to carefully inspect plant roots before buying a tree or shrub. Gently remove the plant from the pot to inspect plant roots, while being careful not to damage the rootball. Healthy plants should slide out of the pot easily (root-bound plants may be harder to examine this way) and the rootball should retain its shape. Ideally, roots will not be circling at the bottom of the container and they will be spread evenly throughout the lower half of the container.

△ Only purchase trees that have been grown with proper positioning in the container. A buried root flare can end up rotting the plant from the ground up.

Most feeder roots are not at the surface, as fertilizer salts tend to accumulate at the surface. If the roots are not holding the soil together, or root growth seems limited, pass on that plant and check another. If all the rootballs look bad, consider choosing another plant, as planting a poorly rooted tree or shrub results in slower growth. However, a plant in which the rootball is a mass of solid roots is not good, either. When you slide the plant up out of its pot, you hope to see roots throughout the container, but soil between the roots should also be evident.

Sometimes roots can circle at the surface if they were watered inconsistently while growing at the nursery. If roots are circling at the surface, inspect the base of the trunk. When roots circle right next to the trunk, the risk of a girdling root increases. Girdling roots can eventually grow into the tree trunk at the base, restricting water and food transportation within the tree. Arborists (tree doctors) see this problem time and time again, and can advise the best solutions if you have a larger tree in your garden with this problem. If it is a small root, ½-inch or less in diameter, you can cut it yourself using a pair of pruners or sharp pruning saw. Be very careful to only cut the girdling root and not the adjacent trunk. Even a small nick can allow insects or disease to enter and harm the tree.

While still in the early phase of adoption at the nursery level, there are containers designed to channel root growth down and prevent circling, girdling roots. These containers may look different than the typical round black plastic pots and they may cost a dollar or two more at retail, but the rewards from buying a tree with a healthy root system are worth the minor increase in cost. If you see trees planted in interesting-looking pots, ask the garden center staff if those containers are "root pruning" type containers to encourage better root growth. You'll sound like an expert and ensure you're getting the best available plant for your garden.

Trees should have a slight flare at the base as opposed to a straight trunk disappearing into the ground. As trees grow larger, the size of the root flare increases to very obvious levels. If no flare is present, odds are good that the tree was planted too deeply in the container and you will need to remove soil from the surface of the pot until you locate the root flare. If, when shopping, you find that the root flare is halfway down in the pot, you should pick another tree. The root flare should be exposed at all times for healthy growth. When root flares are buried in soil, the risk of infection by pests and diseases will increase.

Disease Resistance

Plant diseases can be a major problem in any garden, especially the vegetable garden. Both viral and bacterial plant diseases, as well as fungal infections, can stay in soil on the previous year's dead leaves and fruit, so a quick clean up in the spring helps remove sources of potential infection. When properly rotating crops, any residual plant debris has time to be incorporated into the soil and broken down by soil microbes. Properly cleaning the vegetable garden each year, planning for proper crop rotations, and making good plant variety selection are the best ways to combat plant diseases.

Many plants have a natural resistance to certain diseases and many hybrids are designed and bred with disease resistance in mind. Pay special attention to the variety descriptions in seed catalogs and on plant tags, as this is where you will see attributes such as disease resistance listed for each seed or plant variety. Disease resistance is not limited to vegetable gardens, as many ornamental plants have also been selected for their ability to resist particular diseases.

Following Proper Cultural Practices

With the right plants selected for the right places, half your battle is won. The rest is in garden management.

PLANTING AT THE CORRECT HEIGHT

Plant trees so that the root flare is approximately 1 to 2 inches above the soil line. For most container-grown trees you're likely to purchase at a garden center, this means the root flare should be about 1 inch above the existing soil surface because some minor settling will occur as the tree grows in the pot. Because tree life should be measured in decades, not years, accounting for this slow settling process when planting at home ensures the tree's root flare will remain above the surrounding soil during the tree's lifetime.

If you discover trees in your garden that do not have a root flare exposed, you can try to gently remove the soil yourself by hand (no sharp tools) or you can call an expert arborist to come look at your tree. Arborists can confirm the presence or absence of a healthy root flare. They have a tool called an air spade that uses compressed air to gently but forcefully remove soil and uncover roots at the base of trees for inspection. Removing any girdling roots and leaving the root flare

1. Dig a hole no deeper than the depth of the rootball but approximately twice as wide.

2. Place the tree in the hole, and adjust the hole depth so that the tree is about 1 inch higher than it was planted in the container. This allows for settling of the soil beneath the tree. Use a shovel handle laid across the hole to help determine the proper depth.

3. Mix equal parts compost with the soil that came out of the planting hole. Shovel in soil around the rootball, pausing to gently tamp down the soil when the hole is half full. Periodically check that the tree trunk is perfectly plumb. Continue filling the hole with loose soil, and gently tamp down again to ensure good contact between the soil and the tree roots. Make sure all roots are covered with soil.

4. Soak the planting area with water. Once the soil has settled, build up a 2- to 3-inch-wide basin around the plant to catch rainfall and irrigation water. But do not build a basin if the soil is very heavy and doesn't drain well.

5. Apply 2 to 3 inches of organic mulch, such as shredded bark or compost, keeping the mulch a few inches away from the trunk.

exposed may be all that is required to fix the problem and increase the lifespan of your tree.

Anything without a single trunk (shrubs, perennials, annuals, tropicals, and so forth) will not have a root flare, but should still be planted with the rootball at approximately the same soil level as that surrounding the planting hole. Burying the crown—the area where the roots meet the stem—of any plant can damage it and reduce growth by blocking stems from growing or holding too much moisture at the plant crown.

Perennial plants should be planted slightly higher than the surrounding soil to make sure the crown stays above the soil line. Just ¼- to ½-inch is plenty of root/crown exposure. Add soil around the plant so it covers exposed roots, yet slopes away from the crown. While this is not as important in annual plants, it still helps to have the plant slightly higher than the surrounding soil. When you are done planting and mulching the area, you should not see any roots above the soil line, and with trees, only a root flare should be showing.

INTERPLANTING: COMPANION PLANTING

One cultural aspect of organic gardening is particular to the veggie garden. Ornamental gardens change over time, but by their very nature are constantly interplanted with companion plants. Vegetable gardens, on the other hand, are typically planted in blocks or rows. These rows are typically kept separated from other plants growing in the veggie garden. However, in many cases, certain plants benefit from having other specific plants as close neighbors. Interplanting, or companion planting, is a highly successful way to increase the amount of food grown in veggie gardens because you do not need to wait for one entire crop to be removed before sowing the next round of seeds or plantings. Interplanting is more common in organic vegetable gardens than it is in traditional gardens.

Carrots and tomatoes are one such example of beneficial interplanting. Start a row of carrots in early spring, and after about a month they will be a nice groundcover, their leaves covering the bed. After a few more weeks, carrot leaves top out at about 18 inches above the soil. Tomato seedlings can be planted in the middle of the carrot row because they will rapidly grow up and over the carrots, and help shield them from the sun as the season progresses. You'll be harvesting the carrots before the tomatoes and as you harvest you create passageways for water to percolate down into the soil, better ensuring hydrated tomatoes.

The *three sisters* garden strategy is similar. This concept involves interplanting corn, beans, and squash. The corn acts as a support for the beans, and the beans fix nitrogen in their roots to build soil fertility. The squash provides a groundcover to help the soil retain moisture and protect the garden from herbivores with their prickly stems and leaves. They all provide food and together create a highly functional and efficient gardening approach.

▷ Prevent pest and disease problems by rotating plant families through locations in the garden.

CROP ROTATION PLAN

First Year Layout

Family 1
e.g., tomatoes, peppers

Family 2
e.g., beans

Family 4
e.g., kale, broccoli

Family 3
e.g., squash, cucumbers

Second Year Layout

Family 4
e.g., kale, broccoli

Family 1
e.g., tomatoes, peppers

Family 3
e.g., squash, cucumbers

Family 2
e.g., beans

Third Year Layout

Family 3
e.g., squash, cucumbers

Family 4
e.g., kale, broccoli

Family 2
e.g., beans

Family 1
e.g., tomatoes, peppers

Fourth Year Layout

Family 2
e.g., beans

Family 3
e.g., squash, cucumbers

Family 1
e.g., tomatoes, peppers

Family 4
e.g., kale, broccoli

SUCCESSION PLANTING

Succession planting refers to the practice of planting seeds of the same plant in successive rounds to extend the harvest season for a particular herb, green, or vegetable. Lettuce is a great example. Instead of planting the entire bed with lettuce all at once, plant one row with seed, wait two weeks, plant another row, and so on until you hit the summer season. This gives you smaller amounts, but spaces out the harvest so you continually have lettuce for the whole spring season and into summer. In large gardens, many other vegetables lend themselves to succession planting.

Ideal plants for succession planting:

- Arugula
- Beans
- Beets
- Carrots
- Cucumbers
- Greens (Mustards, Collards, Asian)
- Lettuce
- Peas
- Radishes
- Turnips

One caveat to interplanting is the limitations it places on crop rotation. Crop rotation is the practice of planting a different family of plants in a garden bed each season. Rotating crops helps to increase yield and reduce disease pressure. To increase yield from one crop to another, farmers will plant a nitrogen-rich crop such as legumes before planting a nitrogen-hungry crop such as corn.

Rotating vegetables in the garden helps to reduce disease incidence. When planning rotations, try to grow at least three different plant families on the same plot before cycling the plot back into the original plant group. For example, from the chart on page 122, you might grow a summer crop of tomatoes and a fall crop of lettuce in year one, then a spring crop of peas and a summer crop of squash in year two. Plant the bed with a cover crop over the winter, then the following spring you can turn under the cover crop and plant tomatoes again, or any other member of the tomato, or Solanaceous, plant family.

SPACING AND AIRFLOW

All seed packets list minimum spacing distance for planting. These guidelines are developed to give the gardener maximum harvest while minimizing the potential for diseases to spread and new gardeners are well advised to follow these recommendations. Over time, you may discover that certain plants can be slightly closer together than the seed packet would indicate, which is a real boon in small gardens.

Plants need good airflow around their leaves. When airflow stagnates due to overplanting, this can lead to a number of foliar fungal diseases. Powdery mildew is a classic example. The more airflow present in a garden, the less chance disease spores have to land, and the lower the humidity level will be around the plants. Decreasing humidity around plants also helps decrease disease incidence. Through experience you'll learn which spacing works best to maximize yield and airflow.

VEGETABLE	PLANT FAMILY
Asparagus	Asparagaceae
Carrots	Apiaceae
Celery	Apiaceae
Cilantro	Apiaceae
Dill	Apiaceae
Parsnips	Apiaceae
Artichoke	Asteraceae
Endive	Asteraceae
Escarole	Asteraceae
Lettuce	Asteraceae
Radicchio	Asteraceae
Broccoli	Brassicaceae
Brussels sprouts	Brassicaceae
Cabbage	Brassicaceae
Cauliflower	Brassicaceae
Collard Greens	Brassicaceae
Kale	Brassicaceae
Mustard	Brassicaceae
Radish	Brassicaceae
Beets	Chenopodiaceae
Spinach	Chenopodiaceae
Swiss chard	Chenopodiaceae
Cucumber	Cucurbitaceae
Gourds	Cucurbitaceae
Melons	Cucurbitaceae
Summer squash	Cucurbitaceae
Watermelon	Cucurbitaceae
Winter squash	Cucurbitaceae
Black-eyed peas	Fabaceae
Green beans	Fabaceae
Lentils	Fabaceae
Peanuts	Fabaceae
Snap peas	Fabaceae
Garlic	Liliaceae
Leeks	Liliaceae
Onions	Liliaceae
Shallots	Liliaceae
Eggplant	Solanaceae
Pepper	Solanaceae
Potato	Solanaceae
Tomatillo	Solanaceae

△ Keep plant leaves dry to avoid spread of bacterial and fungal diseases.

Watering Techniques

The best place to apply water is to the soil, not to plant leaves. In some cases where rains are absent for long periods of time, a plant may benefit from a shower. But foliar diseases can proliferate when leaves are constantly wet due to frequent watering and/or rain. Watering the soil underneath the plant limits splashing and helps to minimize this risk. One exception would be if you are giving a plant a foliar spray of fertilizer, such as when applying a foliar feed solution of soluble kelp and/or worm castings.

Removing Diseased Plants

This is a simple rule: get rid of plant material if the plant is diseased. If your county picks up garden debris to be commercially composted, then give it to them to deal with. Otherwise, throw diseased plants in the trash, and do not add it to your own compost heap. If you try to compost disease-ridden plants, you risk reintroducing the diseases into your garden the following season when you add that compost back into your garden. Many pathogens can survive for years; fungal diseases can be especially persistent. Commercial composting operations can achieve temperatures required to kill off the plant pathogens, whereas backyard compost piles rarely do, and it's best not to tempt fate.

Keeping Clean and Tidy Potting Areas

Clean the potting area regularly. Frequently sweep up all soil and plant debris and disinfect potting surfaces and tools at least once per year with hydrogen peroxide. If you use any other cleaner, just make sure you remove all cleanser residues before resuming potting activities. Keeping these areas clean reduces the potential for infection or contamination.

CLEANING AND REUSING OLD POTS

Growing plants in clay pots is usually better for the plants than using plastic pots. Clay pots allow better gas exchange because they "breathe" better than plastic pots. This breathability comes from the porous nature of the clay. Over time, this porous nature also allows fertilizer salts to soak into and through the clay pot. Fertilizer salt residue shows up as a white film on the outside of the pot. This salt can be scrubbed off before reusing the pot for a new plant, renewing the pot to its original terracotta appearance.

Plastic pots should also be cleaned of old residues before reuse, to remove any debris and potential plant pathogens. Farmers typically soak seed-starting flats in a 10:1 water-to-bleach solution. If you try this bleach disinfectant method, use all necessary protective equipment to keep the solution away from your skin and face. Other farmers will leave flats out in an empty greenhouse in summer. A closed greenhouse can easily reach temperatures above 130°F, which helps destroy plant pathogens that may remain on the plastic flats.

Fabric pots are fairly easy to clean up: just roll the pot sides down to remove the old rootball and old soil. Push the rootball out while pulling down on the sides of the pot. If it is being stubborn, run your gloved hand between the side of the pot and the rootball to disconnect the plant from the fabric pot. After removing all soil and debris, you can wash them, if needed, to remove any remaining materials before reusing them the following season.

07

Fighting Pests and Diseases Naturally

As an organic gardener, you can't just reach for the spray bottle and go after any pest or disease problem whenever one occurs, nor will you need to. Once you begin managing your garden organically, you'll find that eventually most problems resolve themselves. The garden is an incredibly complicated system that's amazing at self-regulating—if we allow it to be. Here's what you need to know to manage pests and diseases naturally.

◁ Let beneficial insects do the work of pest control in the organic garden.

The Disease Triangle

To understand what makes plants susceptible to disease, we must first understand the host and the environmental conditions required for the disease-causing organism or agent to successfully establish itself. The illustration of this relationship between host, pathogen, and environment is called the *disease triangle*. This interrelationship is a delicate balance: without the proper environmental conditions, the pathogen cannot infect the host. Without a host or a pathogen, the disease will not occur. Understanding this relationship helps gardeners keep the balance tipped in their favor. In this chapter, we will explore pests and diseases and the steps gardeners can take to minimize their impacts in the garden.

Nature's Balance

Nature is, in its primary essence, a *polyculture*, a diversity of unique organisms all living together in balance. When the balance of the polyculture tips one way and its diversity is compromised, a disease or pest outbreak can ensue. When we plant monocultures—only one sort of tree in a large grove or only one variety of flower across your entire yard, for example—we invite pest outbreaks.

Many modern farms are monocultures, planted with thousands or tens of thousands of acres of the exact same species (corn, soybeans, wheat, sugar beets, and so forth). It is not practical to suggest we can abandon monocultures overnight. After

DISEASE TRIANGLE

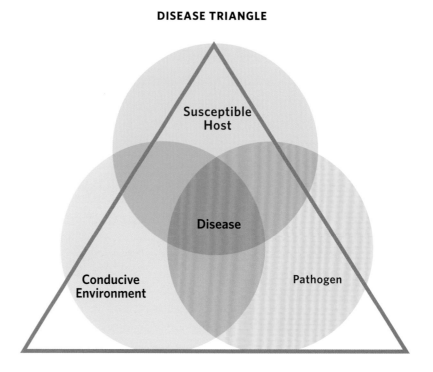

▷ All elements have to be present for disease problems to manifest.

Practical Organic Gardening

△ A garden planted with a variety of species more closely mimics nature and so is more self-regulating when it comes to pests and diseases.

△ The absence of a varied plant and animal community means that monoculture farms can require large inputs of pesticides and herbicides to keep plants healthy.

all, if California farms aren't growing it, how else will people get lettuce year-round in the United States? And in many ways, a fruit orchard can be considered a monoculture. To produce grade-A quality fruit, farmers must spray to protect plants from pests that would otherwise ruin a crop. Most of us will continue to eat locally grown apples produced in this kind of monoculture environment, though we will likely want to take pains to clean the fruit first. But it is also true that this is largely a matter of tradition and habit, and habits can be changed. Learning to eat "ugly" produce may be a small price to pay if it means fewer insecticide applications. Where possible, diversifying from monoculture practices toward the polyculture has benefits, one of which is the reduced need for pesticides.

In our backyard gardens, though, we rarely see a true monoculture environment. While you may have five tomato plants of the same variety in a single patch, or a drift of seven newly planted perennials of the same type, in the big picture these are just multiple organisms grouped together, surrounded by many other unique organisms.

By planting diverse gardens, we provide nature with a base of operations and beneficial insects with a place to thrive. Providing food and habitat is important for birds, but it is equally important for the insect hunters of the garden. These are the "good bugs"—the beetles, spiders, dragonflies, assassin bugs, praying mantids, and

other predatory insects. When you keep an organic garden, these beneficial insects begin to show up on their own because now you likely have their favorite foods present—the "bad" bugs, the insects that eat our plants and annoy us.

It is not uncommon for a gardener to spend years gardening the chemical way, doing battle with specific insect pests only to find that as soon as one is controlled, another equally irritating pest explodes to fill the gap. Once you have shifted to organic methods, though, suddenly the garden may become a balanced ecosystem with an enormous diversity of insects but none that is an overwhelming problem.

△ Praying mantids are valuable predators in the garden, eating insects such as grasshoppers, crickets, flies, moths, butterflies, caterpillars, and beetles.

Insects in the Garden

Insects have a much different way of "seeing" the world than humans. They have developed advanced ways to survive, and while many have eyes to see, they see the world in an infinitely different way than we do. The good bugs are built to search and destroy their prey, using their talents to eliminate garden pests. The bad bugs are searching for plants that meet their particular way of feeding.

Some insects see different light spectrums, such as UV light. Insects can see and/or sense unhealthy plants and choose them as easy targets. Some insects use pheromones to guide them to their prey and sniff out their next meal. In some cases, insects are drawn to healthy plants because they would offer more food resources, and are not drought stressed or otherwise compromised. Some plants, when unhealthy or declining, will exude certain chemical compounds that inadvertently attract insects to feed on the plant, sending that plant into a downward spiral.

On the positive side, plants have also been shown to "communicate" with each other in times of stress, including at the start of a pest outbreak. When an insect starts feeding on leaves or fruit, many plants immediately begin producing chemicals that make it taste unpleasant to the insect. Plants may send chemical messages to other surrounding plants when under stress via increased production of salicylic acid. Other nearby plants pick up on this and begin producing their own salicylic acid as a result. This is but one of the thousands of methods by which plants deploy natural defenses against insect attack.

NATURAL INSECT DETERRENTS

How do we deter these pest insects? There are pesticides we can spray, but what about natural options? It turns out that plants have their own natural defense mechanisms. Many plants naturally contain bitter or toxic leaf chemicals. Some plants, such as tomatoes, have specialized hairs called *trichomes* or other leaf modifications to deter insect pests. Scientists researching these defense mechanisms have discovered naturally occurring pesticides that have been replicated in order to produce some of the pesticides we use today. These are the genuinely organic pesticides.

Some plants are known to produce compounds that repel insects. Citronella is a great example of this. Many a party is ringed with tiki torches spewing citronella-scented smoke into the air. While this is marginally effective, applying repellents to your skin that contain compounds such as citronella is more effective than the smokescreen approach.

You can grow other plants that produce strong-smelling compounds to repel insects, though their effectiveness is limited to the area directly around them. Rosemary, geranium, lemongrass, tea tree, and cedars are good examples of plants that naturally produce insect deterrents. However, most of the oils and compounds have to be distilled to higher concentrations, made into a cream or paste, and applied directly to clothing or skin to afford you protection. It's not enough to just plant the plants.

Integrated Pest Management

The best way to deter insect damage in the garden is to grow a diversity of healthy plants, manage the garden organically, and keep a watchful eye on plant health or the lack thereof in your garden. The process of monitoring plants for insect presence is the science of *integrated pest management* (IPM). IPM involves tracking insect populations and taking action when critical pest levels develop, utilizing effective products that do the least harm to humans and the environment. Back in the 1970s, farmers and growers routinely sprayed pesticides "because it's Friday." We overused pesticides, so much so that insects have evolved resistance to many pesticides that once did the job. Today, most operations use IPM as an important tool to monitor insect populations and take action before pest outbreaks develop.

You can use the principles of IPM at home in your garden. The most important concept is one we can all use—spending more time in the garden looking at your plants. With constant monitoring, we are more likely to catch an insect outbreak at its onset. When pest populations develop, we can take the most effective, least toxic form of control that kills the insects and/or disrupts their reproductive cycle. Time is my first line of defense. For many pest outbreaks, I start by waiting for a week or two to see if the good bugs will show up to eat the bad bugs. Sometimes this works wonderfully and is amazing to behold. Watching lady beetle larvae show up to devour an aphid outbreak is gratifying.

△ Plants just adapt to protect themselves. Trichomes, or tiny hairs on the leaves of tomato plants, are one such adaptation.

△ While watering, weeding, or simply enjoying the garden, keep an eye out for pest or disease problems so that you can address them before they escalate.

Insect Identification

BAD BUGS

Many insects have look-alike traits, so the real culprit might appear to be innocent. Some insects are only active at night or are so quick they easily evade us. Sometimes the best way to identify the insect causing harm is to inspect the damage itself, or the traces left behind by a seemingly invisible pest. Look for insect debris, such as little dark pellets (also known as insect frass or poop), rolled leaves, or specific leaf damage patterns.

Please don't kill insects just because you see them in your garden. Birds need to eat hundreds of insects a day; they will help you keep your garden clean. Until you've identified the caterpillar munching on your plants, leave it for the birds. Who knows: it might just turn out to be a beautiful butterfly.

Once you've identified the insect, you can choose the most effective, least toxic, organic control method. Head to the local garden center to look for organic pest controls. A large garden center should have on-staff experts in the organic controls department. Sometimes the best control method will be a chemical in a bottle, but depending on the pest, sometimes a stream of water is all that's needed to dislodge the insects and send them flying. To a group of aphids, a stream of water is like a water cannon.

A CAUTION REGARDING LADY BEETLES

Lady beetles are perhaps the most widely recognized good bug. However, they are also one of the worst to purchase for release in your garden. Most lady beetles sold in the United States are collected from the wild. While not native (they are originally from Asia), these collected ladybugs spread disease and pathogens around the country, and may end up doing more harm than good.

△ Lady beetles (larval stage shown here) are invaluable beneficial insects.

If you really want to purchase good bugs to release in the garden, look for green lacewings. Even better, make sure you have lots of pollen-producing plants in the garden to naturally attract local ladybugs. Like many other beneficial insects, they need lots of pollen to thrive. Sunflowers, daisies, and other composite flowers are great sources of pollen.

Sometimes, though, you can wait patiently and the good bugs don't show up. At what point do we then reach for other methods of control? The amount of damage we are willing to accept in our gardens is a personal decision. Only you can determine when the insects have crossed the "line in the sand" and merit taking action. For myself, if I see cabbage looper caterpillars on my plants, I don't wait; I immediately remove them by hand.

When bad bugs cross the line, the first step is to correctly identify the problem insect. You can try your hand at researching it yourself. If a quick Google search doesn't turn up my pest, there are reference books to turn to, or your local agricultural extension office. Your local library also likely has many books devoted to the subject.

Sometimes the best control method is one you already have—your fingers. Many insects can be picked off by hand. **Always do your research first, as many insects can bite, sting, or produce chemical compounds that can injure you.** However, many are perfectly safe to pick off and pitch into a container of soapy water. I collect caterpillars on my brassicas (broccoli, cauliflower, and so on) and set them out in a pile on my driveway for birds to eat. They also make a great treat for chickens if you have them! I've collected adult Japanese beetles and potato beetle larvae by the handful and thrown them into soapy water. This method is best to use with slow-moving insects that you can catch off guard.

Of course, these bad bugs don't know they are "bad." Like every living thing, they are simply eating in order to grow and eventually reproduce to complete their life cycle. Insect controls are designed to break up this pattern so the pests cannot reach adulthood and/or so that they cannot mate and lay eggs. If nature isn't doing the job for you and all other control methods fail, it's time to consider using pesticides to kill the pest insect.

▷ Honeybees (top) and hoverflies (bottom) look similar but have different roles in the garden.

INSECT	PLANTS AFFECTED	DAMAGE	PEST LIFE CYCLE/ TIMING OF CONTROLS	CULTURAL TREATMENT	ORGANIC PESTICIDE CONTROL
Hornworms	Tomatoes	Leaves eaten, partial leaves left	Eggs are round, light green, and laid in singles. Remove caterpillars when noticed, unless they are already showing signs of parasitic activity. If cottony ovals are hanging off the caterpillar, it has been parasitized.	Handpick. Cultivate soil lightly after harvest to bring pupae to the surface. Plant pollinator plants to encourage parasitic insects.	*Bacillus thuringiensis* (Bt), naturally occurring biological controls (virus, parasites)
Imported cabbage worms	Primarily brassicas	Irregular holes in leaves	Look for white to yellowish-white butterflies flying around. They have black spots on their wings. They lay eggs that hatch after a few days.	Handpick. Plant pollinator plants to encourage parasitic insects.	*Bacillus thuringiensis*, naturally occurring biological controls (virus, parasites)
Stink bugs	Tomatoes, peppers, brassicas, fruit trees (stone fruit such as cherries, peaches, plums, and apricots)	Blotchy lesions or depressions on fruit, on unripe fruit, small dark dots indicate feeding activity. Affected areas stay green while the rest of the fruit ripens.	Eggs are barrel-shaped and laid in groups. Look for shield-shaped insects crawling around.	Handpick. Keep weedy areas to a minimum to limit stink bug-breeding territory.	Naturally occurring parasitic wasps and parasitic flies
Aphids	All vegetables, fruit trees	Wilting, curled, or distorted leaves; black mold on lower leaves growing on their sugary exudates	Look for small pear-shaped insects, with long skinny legs and antennae, attached to plant stems in colonies. Treat anytime during the year, but only after being patient for a week or two to see if predator insects show up to eat the aphids.	Prune out infected areas. Crush gently with your fingers or spray them off the plant with a strong stream of water. Plant pollinator plants to encourage parasitic insects.	Soap-based products dry out soft-bodied insects. Neem products containing the active ingredient Azadirachtin are also effective

(continued)

(continued from page 135)

INSECT	PLANTS AFFECTED	DAMAGE	PEST LIFE CYCLE/ TIMING OF CONTROLS	CULTURAL TREATMENT	ORGANIC PESTICIDE CONTROL
Flea beetles	Eggplant, peppers, potatoes, brassicas, and corn	Leaves riddled with small holes, large infestations will demolish entire leaves, leaving behind the skeletal leaf structure.	Cover young plants to exclude flea beetles. Older plants can grow faster than damage occurs.	Use a protective row cover while plants are young. Keep weedy areas to a minimum to limit flea beetle breeding territory.	Azadirachtin (need seed extract). Will disrupt flea beetle life cycle causing populations to decrease.
Cucumber beetles	All cucurbits, corn, potatoes, tomatoes, eggplant, beans, peas, beets, asparagus, cabbage, lettuce, and stone fruit trees	Holes in leaves. Skeletonized leaves. Flowers and pollen eaten.	Look for yellow/ orange eggs on stems near the base of the plant. Larvae burrow into soil, eat roots, and emerge as adults after 2-6 weeks. Adults are yellowish green with a black head and black stripes running lengthwise along their body.	Exclude insects from young plants. Protect young plants with row cover or similar.	Surround (kaolin clay solution) protects young plants with a sticky barrier.
Squash bugs	All cucurbits, especially squash and pumpkins	Leaves wilt and/or vines die back from the growing tip. Affected leaves turn black and dry up.	Bronze, elliptical-shaped eggs are laid in groups in spring through late-summer. Treat throughout spring and summer.	Find the eggs and crush them. Place boards in the garden; turn the board over every morning and vacuum up the bugs that were collected underneath the boards. Plant pollinator plants to encourage parasitic insects.	Spray with Neem oil.
Leafminers	Leafy vegetables, apples, pears	Irregular trails are "traced" onto leaf surface.	This is the larval stage of many garden insects. They feed just beneath the leaf surface leaving a trail behind them.	Protective row cover while plants are young. Plant pollinator plants to encourage parasitic insects.	Azadirachtin (need seed extract). Will disrupt leafminer life cycle causing populations to decrease.

INSECT	PLANTS AFFECTED	DAMAGE	PEST LIFE CYCLE/ TIMING OF CONTROLS	CULTURAL TREATMENT	ORGANIC PESTICIDE CONTROL
Root knot nematodes	Most vegetables, fruiting plants	Root galls (swellings), weakened root systems cause slower plant growth and plants often wilt during the day.	Short life cycle, 21-28 days for many species. More abundant in warm and sandy soils. Use control methods year-round for best results.	Divide up the farmland into several sections. Rotate crops and treatments through sections. Treatments to include fumigation, solarization, and a fallow period.	Beneficial nematode applications. Specific compost tea applications with compost tea made to increase beneficial nematode diversity and abundance.
Slugs and snails	Leafy vegetables	Leaves eaten, irregular damage along leaf edge. Can cause serious damage to seedlings.	Control at all stages. Reduce shaded hiding places to reduce slug and snail habitat.	Exclude these pests by using copper barriers. Repel slugs with pelletized wool (Slug Gone).	Look for OMRI-listed products containing iron phosphate. Can place cups of beer at soil level; slugs are attracted to the beer, fall into the cup, and drown.
Scale	Fruit and nut trees, grapes	Overall plant decline. Scale insects produce sticky "honeydew," and, just like aphids, exudate residue, cause outbreaks of sooty mold, and attract ants.	Spray plants when dormant and not actively growing in early spring. This timing coincides with spring egg hatches. **Note:** Dead scale covers can remain on twigs and branches for a long time. Emergent holes on scale bodies indicate parasites are present.	Handpick to remove scale bodies.	Horticultural oil sprayed during the dormant season
Whitefly	Many vegetables, citrus	Leaves may appear yellow. Sap-sucking insects infest plants and produce sticky "honeydew" that can breed sooty mold, just like scale and aphid insects.	Laid as eggs, whitefly rapidly grow to adult stage. Control at all stages.	Remove heavily infested branches. Plant pollinator plants to encourage natural parasitic insects.	Insecticidal soap, and/or a small handheld vacuum. Use the vacuum to suck up the insects in the early morning when they are more sluggish.

GOOD BUGS

We reviewed the most prevalent destructive insects in the veggie garden but we also need to pay homage to the good bugs that help protect our gardens. These include spiders, dragonflies, assassin bugs, praying mantises, wasps, lacewings, minute pirate bugs, aphid midges, some species of beetles and flies, and other predatory or parasitoid insects. These insects are the heroes in the garden, as they consume and kill bad bugs. The spider and praying mantis are perhaps the most well-known predators, but the lesser-known ones, like assassin bugs, dragonflies, and parasitoid wasps, deserve our thanks as well.

Assassin bugs are stealthy, visiting gardens in search of insects to eat. Their powerful piercing-sucking mouth is a long tube called a *proboscis*, which they insert into their prey to suck out the juices. Don't try to pick up the assassin bug or it may pierce your skin while defending itself, and it can be quite painful!

Dragonflies are voracious predators, eating up to a few hundred mosquitoes per day. Certain wasp species also are parasitoids. Parasitoid insects infect their insect host species, usually laid as eggs by an opportunistic mother insect. After the parasitoid species hatches inside the host insect, the parasitoid larvae eat the host insect from the inside out, killing the host insect pest problem. Braconid wasps are one such type that benefits tomato growers everywhere.

🌱 THE HEROIC PARASITIC WASP

The relationship between the tomato hornworm and the braconid wasp is a classic example of a host and parasitoid. Tomato hornworms show up every year in our garden. You can tell they've arrived when you notice missing leaves. Examine the plant long enough and you'll see their green bodies hugging a leaf or stem. If you see small, white, cottony things hanging off their bodies, you are in luck! Those little white things are actually cocoons of braconid wasps. The mother wasp lays her eggs inside the hornworm and the larvae then eat the caterpillar from the inside out. These wasps are tiny and incapable of hurting people, and they should absolutely be left alone. When those baby braconid wasps hatch, they are the next generation of defense against new baby tomato hornworms.

▷ This tomato hornworm has been parasitized by braconid wasp.

△ Green lacewing

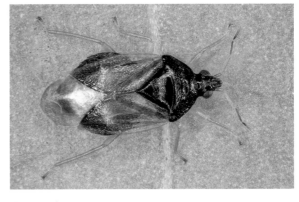

△ Pirate bug

△ Lady beetle

△ Soldier beetle

△ Tachinid fly

△ Praying mantid

△ Black scavenger fly

△ Ground beetle

Insect Control Methods

PESTICIDES

Technically, a pesticide is any substance that kills a target pest, not necessarily just an insect. By a broad definition, pesticides are chemicals specifically formulated to control weeds, microbes, or insects. Sometimes they are broad spectrum and sometimes they are target specific.

Herbicides, rodenticides, fungicides, and other microbial inhibitors are specific types of pesticides. In practical terms, though, the term pesticide is usually used to mean a substance used to control or eradicate insect pests.

There are pesticides that are approved for use on organic farms but they are always used as a method of last resort when all other control methods fail. Broad-spectrum pesticides have the greatest potential to hurt populations of beneficial insects because they are not selective: they kill both bad and good insects. Certain broad-spectrum pesticides are used widely by farmers, and scientific research has shown broad-spectrum pesticide use is linked to such problems as colony collapse disorder among bees. Because bees pollinate fully one-third of all food we eat, it is critically important we do what we can to reverse the trend of declining bee populations—for both farmed bees and native bees.

Your hands are the best tools to remove most pest insects. The next least toxic solution is water. Try blasting the pests off the plant; it may take more than one blast to control the pest. Don't forget to hit the stems and undersides of the leaves as well.

△ The re-entry period is a measure of time indicating when it is safe to re-enter a garden or greenhouse after spraying.

△ Plants dusted with *Bacillus thuringiensis* to control insect damage.

TIMING, OPTIONS, AND BEST METHODS FOR PESTICIDE APPLICATION

Unless it specifically states otherwise on the label, spray pesticides early in the morning for best results. Always take the necessary precautions to avoid coming in contact with the pesticide. Wear long sleeves and pants to cover as much skin as possible. Wear a hat if you can. Get proper gloves and eyewear to protect your hands and eyes. Never spray when it's windy outside. Be careful. Read the entire pesticide label so you know how to use it, and what to do if you or anyone else accidentally comes in contact with it. Always follow the label when determining how long you must avoid the sprayed area before entering it again.

TRAP CROPPING

Trap crops are plants grown specifically for insects to devour, planted so that they will leave your precious plants alone. In the garden, I leave at least one grapevine at all times, as the Japanese beetles seem to prefer it over other garden plants. The plants may differ regionally as to what will attract pests. The best way to determine what pests like is to keep your eyes open in the garden and while you are out and about. Your next great discovery may be waiting around the corner.

☘ CONTROLLING WEEDS ORGANICALLY

Weeds are also pests, by our broad definition, and they can also be controlled organically. The best time to control weeds is when they are young and tender. Weeding is not hard when you use a well-designed tool and do it at the appropriate time.

There are many different types of weeders but my favorites are the CobraHead®, the Circlehoe®, or a Winged Weeder. A sharp tool makes quick work of weeds, and when it has an ergonomic handle to save your back, it is worth its weight in garden gold! Use a weeder to get the root of the weed; otherwise, the plant will grow back. Weeding is one of the hardest tasks of the organic garden. So make it easier on yourself and take care of them when they are young and easily controlled so that you don't have to resort to using chemical pesticides.

Greenhouse operators employ this technique by maintaining specific host plants in the greenhouse. The host plant is base camp for certain beneficial insects, giving them a home that provides a consistent food source. These host plants are usually not for sale, but are specific species grown to rear the young beneficial insects in-house. Outdoors in the vegetable garden, you can also grow extra plants so there's room to allow some to go to hungry insects or you can let certain weeds go in specific parts of the garden to provide insect food. Sometimes, the bad bugs would be just as happy munching on "weeds" as on your vegetables.

BARRIER METHODS

Mechanical barriers are a great way to exclude insects from the garden. Row covers, netting, collars, and cloches can help protect plants against insects and less-than-ideal environmental conditions.

△ Row covers are a barrier method of insect protection.

△ Use nets to protect berry harvests from birds and small mammals.

- **Row covers.** A row cover is a layer of material that covers plants and offers protection from low temperatures and insects. The basic form of row cover is white plastic. High-end row cover material is made by the Gore Corporation. It looks like a thin, white fiber blanket and acts as an insulation blanket that still breathes, allowing air exchange between the plants and the outside. Row cover material can be purchased at local garden centers or through seed companies. You'll also need wire loops to stick into soil over the row; they hold the row cover above the plants. Once set up, row covers look like mini-greenhouses.

- **Netting.** Make sure you're buying netting for garden purposes, and not for protecting buildings. The weights and netting size gauge can be very different. Mesh size and weight can differ when made for deterring specific-size birds. Netting is made from black, thinly woven nylon that, just like it sounds, looks like a net when spread out over your precious fruiting plants. Use it to build a protective layer over and around small fruit plants, such as blueberries and raspberries. The netting prevents birds from taking all your ripe, delicious berries! If you want a decent harvest off your plants, use netting to keep the birds at bay.

△ Make your own collars out of paper cups or paper towel tubes to prevent cutworms from munching young plant stems.

△ Cloches protect plants from pests and late season cold snaps.

- **Collars.** Collars are fashioned around the base of young, tender plants to exclude certain insects such as cutworms. You can use toilet paper or paper towel tubes as collars. When plants are small, gently fold up the leaves so they are in one central column, then simply slip the collar over the leaves so the collar can sit directly on the soil with the leaves coming through the top of the collar. For best results, bury the bottom ½ inch of the collar in soil. You only need 2 to 3 inches of collar to protect the plant.

- **Cloches.** Cloches are a covering that goes over a plant in early spring to protect tender plants from cold or windy nights. I use gallon milk jugs in my garden as cloches. Simply cut off the bottom of the gallon jug and place it over the tender plant. Dig the base of the cloche about ½ inch under the soil line to help it stay put in windy conditions. Save the lid from the jug, as you'll need it on to complete the greenhouse effect. I remove the lids during the daytime so heat doesn't build up inside the cloches.

Plant Diseases

In addition to insect damage, many physiological symptoms in plants fall under the category of diseases, which can be caused by bacteria, viruses, or fungi—the same causes of diseases in humans. Identifying plant diseases can seem a daunting task; however, by paying close attention to damage, you may be able to narrow the culprits down to a short list. Once you take other environmental factors into account, you can make your final determination.

Some physiological problems can cause symptoms that mimic plant disease symptoms. These problems can be due to natural or man-made conditions, such as drought, nutrient deficiency, pollution poisoning, salt damage, cold-induced injury, heat-induced injury, and/or herbicide drift. The abiotic factor should always be ruled out first. Examine the plant, and think about everything in its environment. Ask yourself, could anything other than disease cause this problem?

△ Bacterial wilt is common in cucurbits, such as melons, squash, and cucumbers. It affects plants early in the season.

△ Rusts are fungal diseases that present as rusty-colored spots on plant leaves.

△ Late blight, caused by the fungus *Phytophthora infestans*, affects tomatoes and potatoes (both members of the nightshade family). Crop rotation, practicing good sanitation in the garden, and planting resistant cultivars are the most effective ways to manage this problem.

DISEASE CONTROLS AND TREATMENTS

If in doubt about the diagnosis, cut off an affected leaf and/or stem, place it inside a plastic zipper bag, and take it to your local garden center or cooperative extension office to confirm the disease culprit. Once identified, you can choose the best route forward. Sometimes you can successfully treat the affected plant with a chemical option; other times, treatment requires heavy pruning or removal of the infected plant. The following table summarizes the most common disease pressures of the veggie garden.

As with many garden problems, the best disease control method is cultural control. For fruit trees, bushes, or vines, that means always removing the previous year's fruit that fell to the ground, as this is usually the source of reinfection during the following spring. These fruits and leaves can be burned or sent out to a commercial composting facility for proper disposal.

COMMON PLANT DISEASES AND ORGANIC CONTROL SOLUTIONS

DISEASE TYPE	PLANTS AFFECTED	DAMAGE	LIFE CYCLE/ TIMING OF CONTROLS	CULTURAL CONTROLS	ORGANIC PESTICIDE CONTROL
Verticillium wilt	Many plants, especially tomatoes, potatoes, peppers, and melons	Plants wilt and do not recover because the organism enters the vascular tissue and plugs it up. Eventually plants die. When cut and examined, infected plant stems are discolored and brown.	Fungal spores in soil germinate when nearby roots secrete exudates. Germinated spores enter root tissue through wound sites. Once they enter plant xylem tissue, they reproduce and infect the entire plant.	Solarization can be used to reduce pathogens in soil. Clean pruners between uses to reduce pathogens on tools.	Plant resistant varieties when available.
Rusts	Obligate parasite with specific hosts. Examples: Cedar-apple rust or Bean rust	Leaves get rusty, reddish-brown lesions. Severe on grain crops. Many species can still grow with a rust infection but yield will likely be affected.	Rusts require a host at all times. Fungal spores released in spring land on host plants and germinate. Some rusts, such as cedar-apple rust, require alternate hosts to complete their life cycle.	Remove infested plants, and destroy them by burning or throw them away.	Plant resistant varieties when available.

(continued)

(continued from page 145)

DISEASE TYPE	PLANTS AFFECTED	DAMAGE	LIFE CYCLE/ TIMING OF CONTROLS	CULTURAL CONTROLS	ORGANIC PESTICIDE CONTROL
Late blight	Tomatoes, potatoes	Leaves turn grayish brown. Lower side of leaf has white fungal growth. Leaves and stems will eventually die.	Fungal spores are spread by wind and rain. Onset is usually late summer. Maintain good air circulation around plants.	Remove volunteer plants that may have overwintered the fungus. Avoid sprinkler irrigation so leaves stay dry as much as possible. Maintain adequate soil moisture. Destroy all tomato and potato plant debris after harvest.	Because it happens at the end of the season, the best control is to remove affected plants to slow the spread of disease in your garden.
Phytophthora root rot and crown rot	Many vegetables, fruit and nut trees, and ornamental plants	Plants look drought-stressed. Symptoms may occur on one branch, then spread to the rest of the plant. Plants may die rapidly or decline slowly depending on disease severity.	Fungus thrives in wet, poorly drained soil. Spores present in soil can enter healthy plant roots. Rain and irrigation spread the spores in the garden.	Avoid overwatering and consistently wet soil. Rotate crops to reduce disease pressure.	Plant resistant varieties when available.
Bacterial canker	Many fruit tree species	Irregular-shaped dark lesions on young bark, sometimes accompanied by a gummy substance produced by the bacteria.	Bacterial disease infects plants when conditions are favorable, usually in early spring or in fall. Can enter plants through any opening, natural or pruned.	Provide adequate fertilizer and water for plants.	Select trees grown on resistant rootstocks when available.
Mildew and powdery mildew	Many plant species, including all cucurbits	Leaves covered in white fungal spore growth. Looks like there is powdered sugar on your plants. Affected plant parts yellow, die, and fall off.	Fungal spores survive on nearby weeds, plant stems, leaves, bark, or even inside dormant buds. Spores are carried by wind. Moderate temperatures and shade encourage powdery mildew.	Encourage good air circulation. Plant in unshaded areas. Avoid excess fertilizer. Provide adequate water; stressed plants are more easily infected. Prune out infected leaves at disease onset to delay establishment. Throw away infected plant parts.	Use fungicide sprays containing sulfur and/or surfactants. Look for sprays with the OMRI listed symbol to ensure a fungicide that is approved for use on organic gardens.

DISEASE TYPE	PLANTS AFFECTED	DAMAGE	LIFE CYCLE/ TIMING OF CONTROLS	CULTURAL CONTROLS	ORGANIC PESTICIDE CONTROL
Damping off	Seedlings	Seedling stems will look like they have been pinched at the soil line. Seedlings collapse and die.	Fungi are the cause of this affliction. These fungi are more prevalent in cold, wet soil.	Plant when temperatures are suitable for the seeds being planted. Use well-composted materials. Encourage good air circulation among seedlings. Avoid too much nitrogen while plants are tiny. Solarization can be used to reduce pathogens in soil.	Use fungicide sprays containing sulfur and/or surfactants. Look for sprays with the OMRI-listed symbol to ensure a fungicide that is approved for use on organic gardens.
Crown gall	Fruit trees and shrubs, ornamental plants	Galls develop on large roots near the crown or root flare. Larger plants may tolerate galls. Younger plants can be girdled and killed by developing gall tissue.	This bacterial disease survives in soil on weed roots. Treat infected plants anytime.	Avoid damaging plant roots, especially those closest to the trunk, crown, and root flare. Clean pruners inbetween uses to reduce pathogens on tools.	A biological control agent is available for many crops, but requires treatment at planting time to be effective.
Mosaic virus	Many plant species	Light green, yellow, or white mottling patterns on plant leaves. Patterns usually irregular. Leaves may be distorted and misshapen.	Virus transmission is usually by insects feeding on infected plants, then transferring the virus to new plants. Plant sap can also transfer the virus.	Rotate crops appropriately to reduce virus presence in the garden. Clean pruners between uses to reduce pathogens on tools.	Plant resistant varieties when plant species are known to be susceptible.

△ Root knot nematodes limit plants' ability to absorb water and nutrients, causing stunted growth and wilting. These pathogens can be present in the soil, but are much more prevalent in the warm southern US. Growing plants hydroponically is a work-around.

△ Canker diseases most often affect trees and shrubs, weakening the structural integrity of the plants.

△ Anthracnose diseases affect mostly ornamental plants, including trees, shrubs, and lawns.

△ Black spot is a fungal disease that frequently plagues rose plants. Good hygiene is the best control method. Always remove fallen rose leaves and flower debris to remove inoculation sources.

△ Tobacco mosaic virus affects plants in multiple families. Symptoms present as yellowing or brown blotchy patterns on leaves.

△ Cucumber mosaic virus causes cells to break down, leading parts of the leaf to turn yellow after being infected with the virus. Cucumbers growing on infected plants become misshapen. Plants will begin to appear stunted and flower production will decrease.

Solarization. Solarization is a natural method of pest, weed, and disease control. It involves placing a sheet of plastic over the area to be solarized, anchoring the plastic down tightly against the soil, and leaving it in place for at least 4 to 6 weeks as heat builds up under the plastic layer. The top 6 inches of soil will have the greatest effect from solarizing, as depths below 6 inches do not get as hot.

Clear plastic is the best choice as it allows the most amount of heat to build up in the soil surface. Make sure to remove all vegetation, rake the bed evenly, then irrigate the soil to a 6-inch depth before applying the plastic. This produces a relatively smooth surface that ensures close contact between soil and plastic layer and irrigating helps the process, as moistened soils will heat up faster than dry soils. Bury the edges of the plastic sheet to keep the plastic tight against the ground for best results. Summer solarization periods are the most effective as the sun has the best angle for heating then.

Fungicide applications. Some plant diseases can be cured or at least mitigated with a fungicide application. If you determine you have a fungal problem and decide you're going to go nuclear on it, always use personal protective equipment and follow the directions on the label.

Large Garden Pests: Identification and Treatment

Deer, rabbits, groundhogs, moles, voles, squirrels, chipmunks, and birds: all these animals can be fascinating when viewed as wildlife, but they can also wreak havoc in the garden. Hungry animals will eat your plants down to nubs. If you don't see the culprits but your garden has been attacked, look at the leaves. Deer leave clean cuts, removing entire branches or leaves from the plant. Rabbits and groundhogs leave ragged edges where they rip and tear leaves off plants. If the soil is disturbed near the plant, the culprit is probably moles or voles. If fruit is missing or shaken off the plant and is lying on the ground, it's likely squirrels, chipmunks, or birds.

There are many repellants for leaf-munching animals, such as deer, rabbits, and groundhogs. These repellants are proven to work, but require multiple applications per season for good control, some as often as once per week, and the products are not cheap.

I prefer to exclude the deer from my garden using fencing. Larger gardens need a minimum 6-foot-tall fence to keep out jumping deer. Deer fencing can be purchased or installed by professionals, but occasionally deer will learn to jump over even good fences. Deer are skittish and don't like to enter areas they cannot see into, or in which they cannot see a way out of. Tall hedges make good deer deterrents as well.

Chicken wire or hog fencing is available at your local hardware store to keep out smaller pests, such as rabbits or groundhogs. You'll need stakes to hold up the wire and you should bury the fence deep enough to block out burrowing animals. Build a gate into the garden area; otherwise, you'll have to take the fencing apart every time you need to enter the area.

△ Fences must be a minimum of 6′ tall to exclude deer, although 8′ is even better.

Raised beds are easier to protect, as you simply wrap the fencing tightly around the beds, then slide in a stake to connect the two ends of the fencing together. For deer, I also place bamboo stakes in the bed, pointed up and outward toward any tender, curious deer noses. In my garden, this technique has, for the most part, kept deer at bay for years.

Moles and voles differ in their eating and nesting habits but they both can cause significant damage in the garden. Moles tunnel underground, eating worms, grubs, and insects, while voles live above ground targeting tender plant parts for their meals, but will certainly uproot bulbs and roots for dinner.

Mole damage usually reveals itself where a ridge of soil is raised up from where they have built tunnels under the surface. If you're unsure if it's a mole tunnel, step on it; on mole tunnels, the soil will seem soft underfoot as it tamps back down. To repel these varmints from the garden, you can use a castor oil product to prevent the grubs that are the mole's main diet item. Generally, moles will flee after a castor oil treatment. You can also purchase traps to catch and release moles in wild areas far away from your garden. There are also, of course, killing traps that can be used on moles if your conscience allows their use.

Squirrels, chipmunks, and birds are crafty, quick, and seemingly unstoppable. They can climb or fly over fencing, they are small, and seemingly never full. You can pass a bush in the morning thinking how ripe and beautiful your berries look, and then the next day the plant is entirely stripped of fruit! Netting is the best control to exclude critters from your garden. There are squirrel and chipmunk repellants on the market if you want to try them. There are also live traps that allow you to relocate these animals far away from your garden.

Some states and local laws may prevent you from trapping or killing certain wildlife. Always check with your local jurisdiction to avoid fines or potential jail time. If you end up with a situation where you have endangered species present and bothering your crops and you can make life difficult enough for them, they will find other places to live and eat. Or you can consider planting plants just for them, but on the edges of your property. Then high-five your friends because you have endangered species living on your property!

The following table shows plant groups you can try in order to benefit wildlife in your garden.

❧ BENEFICIAL PLANTS FOR ATTRACTING POLLINATORS AND OTHER WILDLIFE

PLANT GROUPS	
Pollinator-friendly plants	Anything in the Asteraceae plant family with composite, daisy-like flowers. Also, Phacelia, Salvia, Hydrangea, Ceanothus, Conoclinium, Monarda, Agastache, Apocynum, Baptisia, Lobelia, Lonicera, Penstemon, Tradescantia, Verbena, Veronicastrum, Zizia
Larval food sources for butterflies	Anything in the Umbelliferae plant family (carrot, parsley, fennel, dill, Queen Anne's lace), Lindera, Asimina, Quercus, Aristolochia, Salix, Cassia, Asclepias, Lupinus, Plantago, Viola, Prunus, Populus, Rhus, Aster, Chelone, Verbena, Sassafras, Cornus
Berries for attracting wildlife	Lindera, Ilex, Viburnum, Cornus, Magnolia, Aronia, Rhus, Juniperus, Malus, Vaccinium, Callicarpa, Amelanchier, Sambucus, Rubus, Morus, Prunus
Habitat for insect predators	Anything in the Asteraceae plant family with composite, daisy-like flowers. Anything in the Umbelliferaceae plant family (carrots, parsley, fennel, dill, Queen Anne's lace.) Also, Buckwheat, Allium, Agastache, Monarda

08

Propagating Plants Organically

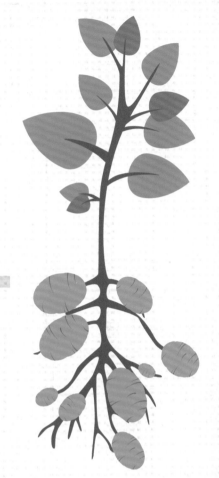

Plants naturally propagate themselves organically, most commonly through spreading their own seeds, but also through vegetative reproduction. When we encourage this vegetative propagation deliberately in our gardens, we call this process "layering" and "taking cuttings." In the wild, propagation through layering takes place when a piece of a plant gets knocked over or falls over and sprouts roots where the stem meets the ground. Propagation through cuttings in the wild happens when a piece of plant breaks off and roots where it landed.

In this chapter, you will learn how to select the right seeds for your organic garden, how to save and store seeds from year to year, how to start seeds, and how to take and grow cuttings. Organic gardening, like all gardening, starts with the seeds.

◁ It's fun and rewarding to propagate your own plants.
Plus, if you grow them, you can be certain they are organic.

153

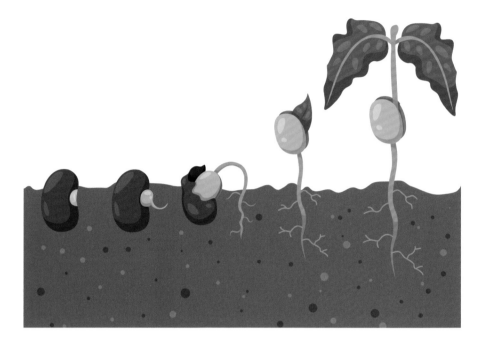

▷ Seeds rely on internal reserves when they first sprout. Once they push out their first true leaves, they rapidly grow into the surrounding soil looking for nutrients and water.

Seeds

Seeds populate even the most rugged patches of newly formed earth: lava flows, mudslides, and post-hurricane landscapes. They push forth, make new life, and blaze trails. Seeds are hope. Seeds are pioneers. Seeds are chance. Each seed has its own unique genetic code, changing slightly with each new generation, yet each retaining the original parent's genetic information.

FRUIT TYPES AND THEIR SEEDS

Growing plants from seeds requires knowing the various mechanisms that produce seed. Some seeds, such as those produced inside fleshy fruit, must go through a fermentation process to completely mature. That process occurs either in the belly of an animal who has eaten the fruit or inside the fruit as the exterior breaks down into a fermenting—and smelly—mess. Many fermenting fruits smell awful but this fermentation process is necessary: it helps to break down the seed coating, which in turn makes it possible for these types of seeds to germinate when conditions are right. Examples of fleshy fruit include apples, pears, blackberries, persimmons, pawpaws, tomatoes, squash, and cucumbers.

All seeds are found in a plant's fruit. Here the term "fruit" is used as a generic term meaning whatever plant structure results from flowering after pollination. "Fruit" can have a variety of forms, not all of them fitting our classic understanding of soft, edible structures. Some seeds are borne in capsules, for example. A capsule is a term to describe a dry fruit, otherwise known as a seedpod. Each chamber in a capsule is called a *locule*, which is where the seeds are found. Capsules contain

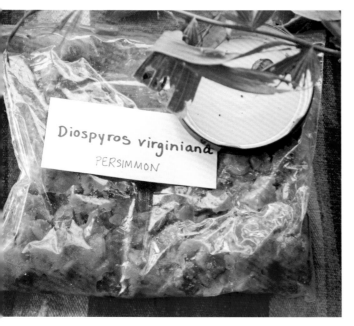

△ Persimmon seeds fermenting

△ Lotus pods and seeds

🌱 THE UNUSUAL FIG FRUIT

A most interesting multiple fruit is the fig. Figs are inverted flowers, in which the flowers are found on the inside of the fruit. The little hole on the end of the fig allows a tiny wasp to enter the flower to pollinate it from the inside. These wasps are so tiny you've likely never seen them and they certainly do not pose any threat to people.

△ Fig flowers are found inside of the fruit.

△ Wasps enter the fruits to pollinate the fig flowers.

many seeds, as contrasted to a nut, for example, a type of fruit in which there is usually just one seed.

Beans are not capsules, but rather *legumes*, but they finish their life cycle as a dry fruit because they split open on two sides to reveal the seeds inside. Berries are the ultimate fruit conundrum, as they are a collection of *drupes* (a type of fleshy fruit), or an aggregate fruit. Blackberries and raspberries fit into this category. Then there are *multiple fruits*, meaning many flowers are fused together into one giant fruit. One common example is the fig.

The terms used to describe fruits may sound obscure, but they are relevant if you wish to harvest seeds and propagate new plants from them. Unless the seed is an F-1 hybrid produced by a breeding initiative and purchased in a store or seed catalog, any time you start plants from seed you collected, you may end up with a variety of results. Some will look like the original plant parents but others may look nothing at all like the parent plants. This is due to a variety of genetic combinations that can occur during seed fertilization.

Gregor Mendel, while working with peas in his monastic garden in the mid-1800s, was the first plant breeder to figure out that there are genetic recombinations during reproduction that affect offspring. His work came to be known as the Mendelian inheritance principle, and is the basis for all plant breeding done today.

△ From the pea flower came the first modern understanding of genetics.

BUYING SEEDS

Spending a morning with coffee or tea and a seed catalog is close to nirvana for a gardener in the winter months when all is cold, wet, and gray outside. Not only do seed catalogs provide inspiration and hope during those dark days, many of them are works of art in their own right. Read through the Hudson Valley Seed Library or Happy Cat Farm catalogs: each seed packet is its own unique piece of artwork.

For most of us, buying a standard-size seed packet is fine. Who needs 200 basil plants in a garden? But if you're looking for bulk options at bulk pricing, look for the seed companies that typically sell to farmers.

Seeds are measured by their percent germination (this data is listed on the seed packs), and are always packed for the year in which they are sold. For instance, packs may say, "Packed for 2018." Old seed won't germinate as well as fresh seed. In my experience, it's worth the money to buy fresh seed each year, though you can store seeds yourself at home under proper conditions (more on that later). Take note of all details provided in the seed catalog (or seed packet), as these details provide important information about planting and harvest times, spacing between

🌱 THE WONDER OF SEEDS

Opening a packet of seeds is always a pleasure to me. Until you know what each species of seed looks like, it's a rite of discovery to open a new pack you've never tried before. Some seeds are long and slender, some are round and bumpy, and some are nearly microscopic.

Seeds come in all shapes and sizes and many of them have specialized parts to help their dispersal. Some fly away on winged appendages (think about maple tree "helicopters") and others may have a sticky barb or coating that latches on to animals (and us) and so get dispersed. Some, such as the seeds of ordinary garden impatiens, "explode" when the ripe seedpod is touched to distribute seed for many feet around the mother plant.

Each attribute of a seed contributes toward plant reproduction. No aspect of a seed's design is an accident. A great way to share seed and expand your plant palate is to check out open-source seed libraries. Just Google "open-source seed library" and begin your fun from there. These resources are a treasure trove of information if you just do a little digging.

△ Seed packets are a wealth of information.

△ Licorice root seeds

plants, flavor, and other unique attributes important for growing that seed.

Additionally, when buying seeds of any kind (vegetable, fruit, herb, woody plant, perennial, or annual), look first for seed companies that are located in the region where you live. These seeds are more regionally adapted to the climate and weather conditions in your garden. However, most gardeners (myself included) will be unable to resist also sampling the offerings from seed companies all over the country. Buying these rarities can be experimental fun and if something catches your eye, go for it. For dependable success, though, buy seeds that were produced in a region close to you. There is a variety of different types of seeds from which to choose.

- **Heirloom seeds.** There are thousands and thousands of seeds available for home gardeners but heirloom seeds have the best stories. While the jury is out on an official definition, heirlooms can generally be defined as those seeds that are handed down from generation to generation. Today, although these seeds may be offered commercially by a seed company, their origin story is one of family and of passing the seed from the previous generation onto the next. The stories may describe unique characteristics exhibited by these precious seeds or sometimes demonstrate how the plant's common name came to be associated with this particular seed. Reading the descriptions in seed catalogs is a great way to learn about the origin stories of specific heirlooms. Heirloom vegetables also have the best flavor in my opinion. Families and communities have collected and passed these seeds down between generations exactly because of those flavors (and shapes and colors). Heirloom harvests are usually not sold in supermarkets and generally speaking, only smaller farms will offer these crops for sale at local farmers markets or co-ops. Heirloom seeds provide a link to our past, and saving these seeds provides food security for our future.

- **Hybrid seed versus open-pollinated seed.** While hybrids can occur at random in nature, the majority of hybrid seed is created when breeders self-pollinate plants to blend the genes from two varieties over and over again for multiple generations. This process, referred to as "hybridization," creates what is known as F-1 hybrids.

The process involves using natural products and processes (pollen and fertilization) to produce plants with new characteristics. Scientists hybridize plants when they see a desirable attribute in one plant and want to incorporate that attribute (such as flavor or disease resistance) with other desirable attributes shown in other plants. The goal, when you cross two plants together that have been self-pollinated for a few generations, is to end up with seeds that will contain the desirable genetic information from both plants.

For example, horticulturists may cross a tomato that tastes great with one that has high resistance to disease. The resulting plant is then back-crossed (self-pollinated) over and over until all the resultant seeds show both desirable characteristics—also known as a *pure line*. This plant is now called an F-1 hybrid. This process usually takes years, which is why most home gardeners leave seed production up to seed companies, or grow open-pollinated heirloom-type seed varieties that do not need such a level of human intervention. Further, seeds from F-1 hybrid plants grown in your garden will not reproduce true to form, because the pollen may or may not have come from the same plant. If you want to continue growing F-1 hybrids from year to year, you generally must purchase new seeds each year.

Open-pollinated (OP) seed is pollinated by insects, birds, bats, humans, or other natural methods, such as wind. Open-pollinated seeds are the most genetically diverse because fertilization happens at random within the species population. You will get even more variation in your resultant seed if you have multiple varieties (or cultivars) of the same species in your garden. To get open-pollinated crops to come back true from seed, you need enough space for blocks of plants, and must make sure they are at least a specified distance from each other. The distance between blocks is different for each seed.

In the home garden, I don't find cross contamination to be an issue. Whether allowed to pollinate at will or tightly controlled to get seed that is true to the par-

🌱 HEIRLOOM PEAS

In my garden, we have saved heirloom pea seeds, both shelling peas and snow peas, for many years. Each year the plants look a little different, but are just as productive as the year before. I try to select the biggest pods on the healthiest plants for seed saving, hoping the majority of the resulting plants will exhibit the larger fruit characteristic just like the original parent plants.

△ Snowpea fruits

Vegetable Isolation Distances for Preserving Open-Pollinated Seed

Seed Type	Isolation Distance	Unit of Measure (UOM)
Arugula	660	feet
Basil	150	feet
Beans	100	feet
Broccoli	660	feet
Beets	0.5	mile
Brussels sprouts	1	mile
Carrots	1,500	feet
Cabbages	1	mile
Cauliflowers	0.5	mile
Celery/Celeriac	1	mile
Chards	0.5	mile
Chives	1	mile
Collards	1	mile
Corn	0.5	mile
Dill	1	mile
Cucumbers	1,500	feet
Eggplants	150	feet
Endives	35	feet
Fennel	0.5	mile
Kale	0.5	mile
Kohlrabi	600	feet
Leeks	1,500	feet
Lettuce	50	feet
Melons	1,500	feet
Mustards	0.5	mile
Okra	1	mile
Onions	1	mile
Parsley	1	mile
Parsnip	600	feet
Peas	50	feet
Peppers	500	feet
Pumpkins	0.5	mile
Radishes	1,500	feet
Rutabagas	600	feet
Spinach	0.5	mile
Summer squash	1,500	feet
Tomatoes	25-100	feet
Turnips	1	mile
Watermelons	0.5	mile
Winter squash	1,500	feet

ent, open-pollinated seeds exhibit variation and will be more locally adapted to your garden. All heirlooms are open pollinated, but not all open-pollinated plants are heirlooms. The definition of heirloom seed generally refers to plants with heritage stories because heirlooms are saved and passed between generations. I am a huge proponent of open-pollinated-type varieties because many of them can be collected in the home garden and re-sown each year.

- **GMO versus GE plants and seeds.** You've likely heard of GMO seeds; the abbreviation stands for genetically modified organism. This term is often confused with GE (genetically engineered), but in order to be on the same page as the USDA and the FDA, we need to have some clarity in terminology.

The media and many other outlets have embraced GMO as a blanket term for GE crops, but there are relevant scientific distinctions between the two terms. Any traditional breeding techniques will create a GMO because it results in a new organism that was created at the hand of a human. GE, on the other hand, requires the use of a "gene gun" or a bacterium called *Agrobacterium tumefaciens* to splice specific foreign genes into the target organism. GE plants have been around since the technology was created in the 1990s, but GMO plants have been around for millennia. Anytime you hear news about GMOs, they are likely referring to GE organisms.

GE technology has resulted in such plants as the much-heralded Golden Rice that has been genetically engineered to produce Vitamin A, which is much-needed by children in developing countries where rice is a staple crop. However, GE plants also include things such as the "terminator gene" (or Genetic Use Restriction Technology), which was developed to inhibit plants from producing viable seed. This ensures that farmers have to buy their seed each year from seed companies, a practice with a great deal of controversy around it.

Many advocates believe that GE needs a lot of ethical oversight to ensure that corporate greed does not undermine the public good and interfere with the ability of people to grow their own food. The ability to save seed in order to grow food the following year is believed by many to be a basic human right that has existed since the advent of agriculture. Organic gardeners in particular need to be well aware of the implications of GE, both the good and the controversial.

If legitimate ethics are considered when designing GE organisms, the science behind them is not much different than that found in traditional plant hybridization. Yes, there are unknowns using GE technology, but there are unknowns in conventional hybridization as well. An organic gardener should be aware of these issues, but it's a mistake to dismiss GE out of hand. If responsibly incorporated into organic farming methods, GE plants may be an important tool to enable the human species to grow enough food to survive in coming centuries.

Some scientists are concerned with the possibility of GE creations, such the terminator gene, escaping through pollen drift and prompting random acts in nature.

For example, if the terminator gene were to escape into other unintended plant species, such as to native forest species anywhere, might it wreak havoc on ecosystems? What if oak trees stopped producing acorns? What if blueberries stopped producing fruit? Such fears might be overblown, but they deserve to be considered.

Another big argument of GE proponents is that they can help reduce the amount of herbicide or pesticides used to grow crops and feed the world. In most cases, this assumption has not borne fruit. In the case of Roundup Ready corn and soybeans, which were created to survive interaction with the chemical glyphosate, the active ingredient in the herbicide Roundup, studies have shown that the number of other herbicides used has only increased since these GE plants hit the market.

But GE has also offered farmers notable successes. A commonly grown GE plant is *Bt* corn, which produces its own pesticide inside the plant itself. *Bt* is shorthand for *Bacillus thuringiensis*, a naturally occurring bacteria that can be sprayed on plants to defend against predation by insects, primarily caterpillars, including corn earworm or other insect larvae that feed on agricultural crops. Once ingested by an insect, the *Bt* bacteria produce crystalline proteins that are toxic to insects. These toxins don't affect people, and *Bt* has been used as a tool for organic farmers to control caterpillar pests for decades. Splice the gene that creates the toxic proteins directly into the corn and now the plant repels the pest, all without spraying pesticide.

The scientific debate about GE seed will no doubt continue, as both sides are passionate about their beliefs. The scientific concept of GE is not necessarily flawed, as any hybridization or breeding work creates a genetically modified organism. However, there are clearly ethical issues involved in GE technology and organic gardeners are well advised to be aware of all the pros and cons.

• **Organic seed.** Many seed companies offer certified organic seed. You'll see the USDA Certified Organic seal on seed packets, as this USDA seal is designated for anything edible, including seed produced from organically grown plants. (The Organic Materials Review Institute (OMRI) seal is only for gardening products—not edible plants or food.)

For your garden to be 100 percent organic, it's important to start with organic seed, or at least untreated seed. Commercially packaged seeds are often treated with a fungicide coating to help protect seeds while in the germinating process. These treatments are usually reserved for seeds destined for large-scale farms or other specific applications. Most non-commercial seed companies do not treat their seeds, as it adds more cost and is not necessary in most cases. Just like many things in life, *au naturel* works just fine.

△ This is the official USDA Certified Organic seal.

△ Garlic chive seedhead ready for harvest.

△ Ramp seed

△ Use cups or small jars to collect seeds and keep plant varieties separate.

Collecting Your Own Seeds

Collecting seed can be a rewarding activity. Dry fruits are the easiest to collect, as the seedpods are ready to pick and store when they are dry. Be aware, though, that some seeds are best harvested when the seedpod has a little moisture left inside, then dried completely in more controlled conditions. Beans are one such example. When left too long on the vine, fully formed bean seeds may dry out, only to be wetted down by a rain shower and then germinate. Once a seed is mature, it can even germinate inside its seedpod if it absorbs too much water while still out in the garden.

If you can hear the seeds rattling inside the seedpod, they are definitely ready to harvest. Take care not to dump out the seed while harvesting it. Placing a white paper towel or plastic container under the flower stalk can help identify and catch any falling seeds. You'll have to watch each plant's flower to determine the perfect timing for harvest, as it is different from plant to plant. Generally, the time to harvest is after the flowers have faded and any resulting seedpod has matured.

Keeping tabs on your plants' "baby factory" pays dividends, as your observations will tell you when the seedpod is mature—perhaps indicated when it has grown to its fullest size, and perhaps by a color change or change in moisture content. When the seed is mature, pick it and place it in a controlled environment to dry down completely before cleaning and storage.

▽ Northern sea oats

△ Before you can dry and save tomato seeds, you have to ferment them to remove any clinging fruit.

CLEANING SEEDS

Cleaning seeds borne inside dry fruits is a relatively easy process, but it can be time consuming. Start by removing all foreign debris—basically anything that is not a seed. Place collected seeds on paper towels inside a bowl or dish to dry out completely before packing for storage. When you're done, you should have pure seed ready to place into labeled packets, small envelopes, or recycled plastic medicine containers until you are ready to plant them in seed-starting trays or directly in the garden.

Cleaning seed borne inside wet, fleshy fruits is a bit more involved, but it's all in the technique. This process, like most in organic gardening, mimics what happens in nature. Basically, you allow seeds to ferment in the juices of their fruits just as they would once they fall to the ground or break down in the belly of an animal. You can remove the seeds and

Seed Type and Seed Longevity If Stored under Proper Conditions

Artichokes	5 years	Corn	2 years	Pansies	2 years
Arugula	3 years	Cucumbers	5 years	Parsley	1 year
Asparagus	3 years	Dill	3 years	Parsnip	1 year
Basil	5 years	Eggplants	3 years	Peas	3 years
Beans	3 years	Endives	5 years	Peppers	2 years
Beets	4 years	Fennel	3 years	Pumpkins	4 years
Broccoli	3 years	Kales	4 years	Radishes	5 years
Brussels sprouts	4 years	Kohlrabi	3 years	Rutabagas	4 years
Cabbages	4 years	Lavender	5 years	Sage	3 years
Calendula	3 years	Leeks	2 years	Savory	3 years
Carrots	3 years	Lemon balm	5 years	Spinach	3 years
Catnip	5 years	Lettuce	6 years	Summer squash	4 years
Cauliflowers	4 years	Melons	5 years	Thyme	3 years
Celery/Celeriac	3 years	Mustards	3 years	Tomatoes	5 years
Chards	4 years	Nasturtium	3 years	Turnips	4 years
Chives	1 year	Okra	2 years	Watercress	5 years
Cilantro	5 years	Onions	1 year	Watermelon	4 years
Collards	5 years	Oregano	2 years	Winter squash	4 years

inner pulp from a fruit and allow it to ferment in a dish on the counter, or you can let it occur inside the fruit itself. Once the fermentation process runs its course, rinsing with water is usually all that is necessary to remove any leftover funky "gunk." You can use a fine strainer for this process so you don't lose precious seeds down the drain. After giving your seeds a bath, remember to let them dry completely on a paper towel before placing them in storage.

STORING SEEDS AT HOME

Gardeners inevitably end up with half packets of seed after sowing a full complement in the garden. We all hate to throw away seeds, but keeping seed viable requires specific conditions to ensure the highest rate of future germination.

Keep seed in a cool (less than 50°F) and dark place, ideally with low humidity (around 40 percent). Under good storage conditions, seed can stay viable for a few years. Seeds vary in their longevity from crop to crop, losing viability as time marches on. Some seeds, such as onion and leeks, are best sowed within one year of collection, while other seeds, including tomatoes, watermelon, and kale, can be stored successfully up to four to five years.

Commercial operations use a seed cooler for storage, but you can replicate these conditions in your refrigerator (not the freezer). Place all seed packets or envelopes in a sealed plastic double zipper bag, and throw in a desiccant pouch to control the humidity/moisture content inside the bag. (I save those desiccant packets found in medications and other products to use specifically for this purpose.) You'll want to replace the desiccant pack about every six months to make sure the humidity content stays near optimal while your seeds are in storage. Don't forget to label each seed packet and place a date on the outer plastic bag, so you know which year the seeds were collected.

In spring, when you are ready to remove your seeds from cold storage and prepare for planting, leave the sealed bag out until it warms to room temperature. This ensures any condensation stays on the outside of the outer bag and will not condense moisture on the seed packets and seeds, as this can affect seed viability and germination rates. Once it warms to room temperature, you can break out your seed and begin planning the spring garden.

Looking beyond the vegetable garden, be aware that some ornamental and/or native plant seeds require a period of cold before they will germinate. The natural cycle of most seeds causes them to develop over spring or summer, ripen in fall, get distributed by nature, then wait patiently through winter before germinating the following spring. Some seed even requires multiple cold cycles before germination. If you save your own seed from native plants for propagation, you can mimic this cold period (known as *stratification*) by placing your collected seed in the refrigerator over winter and sowing the following spring.

Propagating Plants from Seed Indoors or Under Cover

Most seeds can be started outdoors directly in the garden, but, especially in cooler climates, there is an advantage to getting a jump on the season by starting seeds indoors or under greenhouse or cold-frame cover before the garden soil is ready to accept the seeds. This is a key skill for the organic gardener.

TOOLS AND MATERIALS FOR SEED STARTING

- **Soil mix.** When choosing a soil, it pays to look for one that is formulated specifically for seed starting. Seed-starting soil is generally lighter than potting soil, and is made from finer particles that increase the soil-to-seed contact during the critical start of seed germination. While not found in all soils, good ingredients to look for include coconut husk fiber, worm castings, and rice hulls. These ingredients are Earth-friendly and help seeds grow into healthy transplants. Try your local garden center for seed-starting blends: it is sure to have one or more options for you. Many seed-starting blends have a small starter charge of fertilizer included, as young plants benefit from a fertilization boost after about three to four weeks to help them continue growing into healthy-sized transplants.

- **Trays.** There are all kinds of trays for seed starting. When starting seeds for future transplanting, I prefer fiber pots over plastic. The plastic pots are reusable a number of times before they get too brittle, but the biodegradable fiber pots are Earth-friendly and can be planted in the ground with the plant—provided the roots have grown through the pot. Fiber pots may need more water than plastic pots because the fiber pots dry out more quickly in low-humidity conditions (such as inside your home in winter). Plastic pots hold moisture longer in the soil, so if your seedlings are drying out too much, perhaps try a plastic tray with a humidity dome.

- **Heating mats.** If starting seeds early indoors, you may need a little extra heat to get them growing. Seedling heat mats are available in many sizes, from a single flat to larger sizes that can hold three to four flats of seedlings. You can buy temperature control units to dial in your preferred germination temperature and confirm what your seeds are actually receiving.

△ Find seed-starting trays at your local garden center or home improvement store.

△ Using a heat mat under seed-starting trays ensures quick germination and helps prevents problems with damping off.

◁ Using a digital thermostat allows you to control the heat mat's temperature.

THE OMRI STANDARDS

When buying a seed-starting blend look for one with the OMRI-listed seal. OMRI is the Organic Materials Review Institute, an independent third-party certifier of inputs for organic farming. Soils, fertilizer, insect controls, plant growth enhancers, and more can be listed by OMRI if they meet the strict OMRI standards, most of which are equal to standards at USDA-certified organic farms.

OMRI-listed products must be tested for heavy metals, nutrient content, fecal coliform, and salmonella bacteria. Other OMRI requirements include no tolerance for GMO ingredients, sewage sludge, or irradiated products (because these three are not allowed in organic agriculture they are also not allowed in OMRI listed products).

△ A rule of thumb is, "the larger the seed, the deeper it is planted." Plant seeds approximately three times deeper than their widest point. For example, lettuce seeds are about 1mm wide, so they should be planted approximately 3mm deep.

HOW TO START SEEDS INDOORS

There is a classic rule of thumb when planting seeds. Measure the widest point of the seed, and then multiply that measurement by three. The answer is the appropriate depth to plant each seed in the soil. For example, if a seed is 1 millimeter wide (as are basil or lettuce), then it should be planted 3 millimeters deep. If a seed is ¼-inch wide (peas or beans), then it should be planted ¾-inch deep. Don't worry about being slightly too deep or too shallow, but a seed planted substantially too deep will likely not germinate.

If you don't have good natural light, you'll need a germination light. Fluorescent lights make great germination lights and they are inexpensive and readily available. Lights are especially useful if you're starting seeds in a basement or other dark area. While fluorescent lights work, the must be very close to the plant leaves to provide enough light for the seedlings to grow. Fluorescent lights don't produce much heat, so they can be within an inch of plant leaves. Turning a small fan on the little seedlings is also a good idea. It causes seedlings to move a bit, which strengthens up their tiny stems to get them ready for the outside world. Keep the direct brunt of the fan away from the seedlings, though; they only need a gentle breeze for this.

1. Fill a seed-starting tray with soil. Make sure all of the cells are filled in and that the soil is evenly distributed in all cells.

2. Gently smooth out the soil over the tray, making sure each cell is filled.

3. Run your hand over the tray one last time to make sure the soil is at the same level in each cell.

4. Use a small stick to poke holes in the soil to plant them at the appropriate depth.

(continued)

5. Sow two seeds in each fiber pot. This increases your chances to get one good transplant in each cell. You can remove the smaller of the two seedlings if both emerge.

7. Water the seedling trays or pots. No matter which seed-starting pots you choose, the most important thing to do now is keep the seedbed moist. You can use a plant mister for this if you can't take the tray outside to soak the cells, but I prefer watering in seed trays outside with a watering wand on the rain setting and a breaker on the end of a long handle (not the twistable types with different water settings). This "static" watering wand coupled with a brass shut-off valve is my tool of choice when watering seeds or anything in the garden. Use the valve to control the water speed and give your seedlings a light shower as you pass the watering wand over the seed trays. Do this motion quickly to keep the shower from washing out the tiny seeds: they need to stay cocooned in the soil where you planted them.

6. Cover each seed with a bit of soil, and gently but firmly tamp the soil down for good soil to seed contact.

8. Provide heat. Seeds need warm soil to germinate. If starting seeds outdoors, you can construct a propagation bench with a hoop house. Cover the hoops with plastic sheeting or frost protection cloth to give the tender seedlings a miniature greenhouse. You can

◁ If you have a small greenhouse, you can create your own propagation bench.

Sowing Seeds Directly

Many seeds are best sown direct in the garden. Certainly, any seed can be started in trays, but sowing direct into garden soil eliminates a lot of extra time and may result in faster growth. Examples include almost all root crops (beets, carrots, turnips, parsnips, and potatoes). It's still crucial to water consistently during the germination and establishment process. Depending on the time of year, Mother Nature may provide all the rain needed for seed establishment, but use overhead sprinklers or a watering wand to provide irrigation if rain is limited. Follow the seed depth guidelines discussed earlier in this chapter for best results.

I also use a method a friend taught me to sow seeds direct in the garden without any need for seed cleaning and storage. Seeds such as lettuce, carrot, or any other dry seeds borne on flower stalks are ideal for this method. I simply wait until the seed is mature, then cut the plant at the base, and thresh (beat) the plant's seedhead all over the garden area. Seeds will fall off randomly and lodge in the soil, and will then germinate when conditions are right. I do lose some percentage of the seeds to animals (birds, insects, and so forth), and some likely rot before germinating, but by and large, I get a decent number of "naturally" sown plants each year.

After using this method for a few years, the plants begin developing a tolerance to direct sowing and the resulting seeds reflect that. The plants are slowly adapting to the local climate, which will result in hardier seedlings. Because these seeds may germinate early, protection from cold may be required at some point in early

▽ Keep seeds moist after sowing and you will be rewarded with quick growth.

spring. After multiple generations, seeds may develop a tolerance to cold spring temperatures, but until then, watch the weather and check the seedbed occasionally in spring to see when plants begin emerging from winter slumber. Certain species may germinate in late fall, overwinter in soil, and begin growing again in early spring when soil temperatures begin to rise. These plants will provide the first harvest of spring, and serve as a reminder of the bounty to come.

Propagating from Vegetative Cuttings

Propagating plants from cuttings is both thrifty and satisfying. You cut a piece of a plant, root it, and in a few weeks—*voila*! You have a new plant created from the original parent plant. Of course, trial and error will provide good lessons in getting the process down pat. While not all plants are easy to grow from cuttings, many plants do very well with this propagation technique. Here's the beginner's guide to successful propagation by cuttings.

TOOLS AND MATERIALS

Planting tray. For propagating vegetative cuttings, I suggest buying a seed-starting kit, as these can be reused over and over again. Most come with a tray, usually with 72 "cells" into which you'll put your rooting material. Good ones also have a humidity dome for the top of the propagation tray, though most of these domes are too short for large cuttings. You can also find larger humidity domes at hydroponic gardening stores or online.

An alternative to the plastic 72 cell-style tray is to use fiber pots to hold your rooting material. The process of setting up the tray is still the same, but you arrange the fiber pots inside the plastic base, fill them with rooting material, and then place the humidity dome on top after inserting your cuttings. Fiber pots are more Earth-friendly and eventually biodegrade into the soil after planting. These pots are designed to hold up for approximately 2 months while plants are rooting.

Rooting material. The plants must root into something. Some people use pure perlite, while others use rooting blocks of rock wool or well-drained potting soil blend. Sometimes the choice is based on the environmental conditions where the plants will be rooted. What a gardener can do in the home or backyard garden versus large-scale nurseries that propagate thousands of cuttings is different because the conditions are different. Everyone finds their preferred method; each has its own unique set of benefits and challenges.

> ### COMPOST SEEDLINGS
>
> Friends frequently tell me about seedlings they find in their compost pile or vegetable garden. "They were free seedlings!" they exclaim with the same excitement preschoolers reserve for ice cream. If you eat and grow mostly open-pollinated heirloom-type vegetables, then the resulting plants are likely to produce food for you. However, due to genetic diversity, you never know how they'll turn out, and there is a chance they will carry over disease from the previous season. While this level of uncertainty is acceptable with leafy greens, I prefer to grow fruiting plants such as tomatoes from seed so I know exactly which variety I'm going to get and have some assurance that the plants will start out disease-free.

Rooting solution. Rooting solution stimulates root growth. If you want to go 100 percent organic, try using honey as an organic rooting solution—though it does take a bit longer. Honey coats and protects the cutting while the plant assembles its own natural rooting hormones at the base of the new cutting. For a bigger boost and faster rooting, try soaking cuttings in a solution of willow (*Salix* sp.) extract first. Willow trees produce an abundance of naturally occurring rooting extracts that you can use to make your own solution. Take cuttings of new growth from a few willow branches, crush the stem tips and any buds present on the cuttings, and place the crushed stems in water. Let the cuttings steep for at least 4 hours. There is one commercial rooting solution product available from a company called Tappin' Roots® that is made with willow extract. As a bonus, this product can also be used as a general plant stimulant.

Rooting environment. Plants root best when temperatures are warm outside. Spring and summer are generally the best times to take and root cuttings. Don't take cuttings off blooming plants. Cuttings root better when taken from non-blooming plants. Keep your cutting tray with a humidity dome in a shadier spot on your property—full sun may cook the cuttings inside a dome. If in a cooler climate, consider placing a heat mat under the tray to encourage root development.

1. Prepare the rooting dome and propagation tray. Make sure each cell is full of soil. After filling the trays with your choice of rooting material, soak the trays with water so the rooting material is saturated. Now your tray is ready, and it's time to take some cuttings.

2. Select the plant you want to propagate through a cutting. The ideal branch is growing, healthy, and not in flower. Plants that are actively flowering do not root well. Take your leafy stem, and look at the point where the leaves meet the stem—call a *node*. Your cutting should have at least four leaves, but also at least three or four nodes. Cut the branch off the mother plant and stick the cuttings in a glass of water. Mix a little soluble kelp into this water to give the cuttings a little boost.

3. Prepare each cutting by trimming off half of each leaf. This reduces the amount of water lost by transpiration through the leaves while the cutting is rooting, which is important because the cutting is no longer attached to a root system. Depending on your climate, now is a good time to mist your cuttings with water to increase the humidity and help them slow water loss while you are preparing the cutting.

4. Remove leaves on the bottom of the stem, starting at the third node. Then snip the stem neatly with a sharp pair of pruners about ½ inch under the third node. If you don't have a pair of pruners, then use sharp scissors. When you're done, it should be a clean cut. Next, make a second cut on the stem under the node that has no leaves in order to shorten the final stem size down to about ¼ inch.

5. Dip the third node into a rooting solution as directed on the product label. Then stick the cutting gently into the center of one of the cells you created earlier, about halfway to three-quarters of the way down into the cell. Mist the cutting again for good measure. Continue this process until you've prepared and stuck all your cuttings.

6. Gently place the humidity dome on top of the tray. Some nicer humidity domes have a valve you can open to allow for small amounts of air exchange. If so, keep it closed at first, to keep the humidity close to 100 percent under the dome. After the first few days, try opening the valve a little bit and see if anything wilts after a few hours. If no wilting occurs after that period, then leave the valve open to allow for continuous air/gas exchange. As time continues, you will eventually be able to open the valve all the way. Only after the plants have rooted in fairly well can you leave it wide open.

7. Water the cuttings. Watering cuttings is easy while they are rooting, since water is recycled on a daily basis inside a humidity dome, condensing on the sides of the dome and running back down into the bottom of the tray. Domes with closed valves will lose very little water. Propagating in drier conditions may require extra care, but only occasional misting should be needed, about once per day while the cuttings are rooting in the tray. Make sure the leaves are covered by a layer of water droplets when you're done misting the cuttings.

09

Planning Your Organic Garden

The variety of potential organic garden types is staggering, as everyone has different preferences when it comes to plants and reasons for gardening. The principles of organic gardening are the same whether you're into vegetable gardens, herbs, trees, cut flowers, growing your own hops, gardening for wildlife, gardening with children, increasing your curb appeal, entertaining friends, or simply relaxing in the garden. Many of these principles have been discussed in previous chapters. In this chapter, we dive into specific garden types to discuss planning and preparation, installation, and maintenance.

◁ A little planning goes a long way toward growing a productive and pretty garden.

▷ Most people think of vegetables when they think of organic gardening.

▽ Enjoy home brewing? Want an unusual vine? Grow hops!

△ Native plants are just as eye-catching as traditional bedding plants.

Planning and Preparation

No matter what specific subset of plants you're into, all gardens begin with planning and preparation. Start by giving thought to your entire property. What is your primary goal? How can specific objectives achieve that goal? How much space or resources can you allot for each objective?

If this sounds like a pep talk, it is. You have to decide what you truly want out of a garden and then decide whether you have the resources to make it happen. It's your garden, your space; there are no wrong answers, only whittling down the list to what really motivates you to get outside and garden. Once you have decided goals and objectives for your garden, you can create a timeline prioritizing which garden aspects are the most important to begin immediately and which garden projects can be postponed to next year or the year after.

Some people will choose to get trees in the ground first, as they take the longest to mature. Other people opt immediately to break ground on the vegetable garden, herb garden, or cut-flower garden, as they provide immediate gratification and harvests in the first year. Whatever you choose, stick to the plan you created initially to achieve your garden goals, but also allow for fluctuations due to your changing interests or life events.

A plan gives you clear objectives to rely on, so you don't get caught with five different projects all at once. Being unrealistically ambitious can quickly turn your plan into an overwhelming, weedy headache that creates nothing but discouragement.

△ Introduce kids to gardening early and cultivate a lifelong love of plants.

△ Gardens aren't just for producing. They should be places of relaxation too.

I suggest starting by focusing on the areas that are closest to your home. These are the areas you'll see on a daily basis and these areas have the greatest potential impact to improve your quality of life. If you have no yard, this may mean focusing on houseplants to clean the indoor air and beautify your home. For some of you, perhaps the walk from your vehicle to the front door is your primary focus. For others it may be the view from the kitchen window. Regardless, the areas closest to your home will deliver the most tangible results. This concept is the base idea in *permaculture*, a concept that involves gardening with sustainability in mind and using the least amount of energy to get the most out of your garden space.

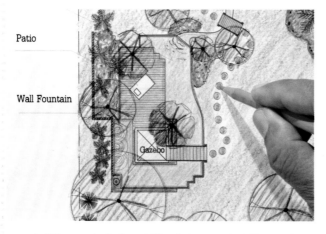

Patio

Wall Fountain

Gazebo

△ When you're in the middle of a large project, it's easy to get overwhelmed. Drawing a simple plan gives you a roadmap to follow, making large-scale garden renovations less stressful.

△ Add life to your deck, patio, or porch with plants.

△ Food forests are productive on the tall, medium, and ground levels of the garden.

Types of Organic Gardens

You'll be most successful as a gardener if you grow the types of plants that you like to eat or enjoy looking at. Here are some ways to combine plants in innovative organic gardens.

Plants for Making Your Own Pet Food	Plants for Cut-Flower Gardens	Plants for Kitchen Gardens (or Jardin Potager)
Amaranth	Amaranth (*Amaranthus*)	**Herbs:** Basil, Bay laurel, Dill, Garlic chives, Fennel, Lavender, Mint, Oregano, Parsley, Rosemary, Sage, Thyme
Cabbage	Aster (*Symphotrichum*)	
Carrots	Bee balm (*Monarda*)	
Clover	Blazing star (*Liatris*)	
Corn	Celosia (*Celosia*)	**Fruits:** Apple, Apricot, Aronia, Banana, Blackberries, Blueberries, Cherry, Cranberries, Figs, Goumi, Grapes, Hardy kiwi, Loquats, Medlar, Paw paw, Pear, Persimmon, Pineapple guava, Plum, Pomegranate, Quince, Raspberries, Sea berries, Strawberries
Green beans	Coneflower (*Echinacea*)	
Lettuce	Cosmos (*Cosmos*)	
Parsley	Crocosmia (*Crocosmia*)	
Peas	Dahlia (*Dahlia*)	
Pumpkin	Gladiolus (*Gladiolus*)	
Sweet potato	Hydrangea (*Hydrangea*)	
Sunflower sprouts	Lady's mantle (*Alchemilla*)	
Wheat grass	Lilac (*Syringa*)	
Winter squash	Lily (*Lilium*)	
	Peony (*Paeonia*)	
	Pincushion flower (*Scabiosa*)	
	Red twig dogwood (*Cornus*)	
	Siberian iris (*Iris*)	
	Speedwell (*Veronica*)	
	Sunflower (*Helianthus*)	
	Tickseed (*Coreopsis*)	
	Zinnia (*Zinnia*)	

FOOD FOREST

The concept of a food forest is just as it sounds: planting a garden with edibles in mind. A food forest has something edible in every layer, from the tallest tree to the ground layer. The canopy layer trees are usually fruit trees, with other smaller fruiting trees or bushes underneath the canopy layer. The ground layer should be perennial crops harvested for their leaves, seeds, or roots. Experimenting with this concept can yield tasty results! Do your research to identify edible crops that will work in your zone and combine well together to create a functioning food forest.

FOOD FOREST LAYERS

Canopy Layer .... Apple, Apricot, Banana, Cherry, Fig, Grapes, Hardy kiwi, Loquat, Pawpaw, Pear, Pecan, Persimmon, Plum, Quince, Sea berries, Walnut

Middle Layer .... Aronia, Asparagus, Bay, Blackberries, Blueberries, Goumi, Hazelnut, Medlar, Pineapple guava, Raspberries

Groundcover .... Alpine strawberry, Arugula, Collards, Cranberries, Creeping rosemary, Kale, Lamb's quarters, Lettuce, Malabar spinach, Mustard, Nettles, Pomegranate, Rocket, Sea kale, Spinach, Strawberries, Sweet potato, Swiss chard, Thyme, Wintergreen

MUSHROOM FARMING

Mushrooms are the tasty fruit of a fungus and they can be grown in any garden. Mushroom kits are increasing in popularity, but these are usually indoor kits. Growing mushrooms in the garden involves buying inoculated plugs from quality suppliers such as Fungi Perfecti and placing the plugs inside newly cut tree limbs. You'll need a drill and a few other supplies, but anyone can make mushroom logs. Detailed instructions come with every purchase. Here are some basics steps. The best type of wood to use varies with mushroom variety.

To build your own mushroom farm:
1. Determine the type of wood that is best for the mushrooms you want to grow (this should be in the package instructions) and find branches or logs that are approximately 4 to 6 inches in diameter.

2. Drill holes approximately 4 to 6 inches apart in the branches, following an offset "dice" pattern around each log. Closer spacing results in faster colonization. Use a drill bit that is only $\frac{1}{32}$-inch larger than the plug diameter. The hole depth should be $\frac{1}{8}$-inch deeper than the plug length.

3. Pound the plugs into the holes. Melt wax and brush it over the plug to protect it from insects or other contamination.

4. Place the mushroom logs in the garden where they can get rained on, then wait. It takes anywhere from 6 months to a year before the chosen fungus can eat its way through the log.

Once the log is completely colonized, it will begin to fruit. Each mushroom type has a preferred temperature range for fruiting. If you don't see fruits after 12 months, soak the log in water for 24 hours to stimulate production. A couple of days of rain is sometimes enough to stimulate mushroom growth naturally. Mushroom logs may continue fruiting for several years, but harvests decrease as time goes on and the logs are consumed.

△ Mushroom logs

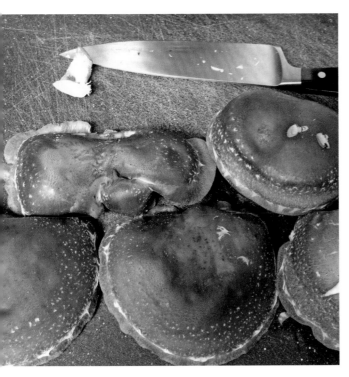

△ At the perfect time of year, each mushroom log can yield multiple pounds per week. Yes, that is a 9-inch chef's knife in the picture for scale!

△ It's great fun to harvest your own mushrooms.

△ Figs ripening on a tree.

VEGETABLE GARDENS

Vegetable gardens are making a backyard resurgence not experienced since the spread of the Victory Garden during World War II. The interest in growing fresh, healthy foods has a variety of instigators:

- Schools are incorporating gardens into educational curriculum at an ever-increasing rate.

- The rising interest in cooking shows such as those on The Food Network has millions of people looking at food like never before.

- For some, growing certain varieties of fruits and vegetables at home is the only way they can get personal favorites that may not be available at the local grocery store or farm market. Other people simply don't have ready access to fresh foods.

- New attention to the effects of healthy eating as a means of curing or preventing disease is at an all-time high and with it an interest in growing chemical-free, healthful vegetables.

For some, the interest lies in using freshly harvested produce in meals to show off their prowess at gardening to their family and friends. Some are keen to join the current foodie movement, using these fresh fruits, veggies, and herbs in everything from homemade craft cocktails to cooking up the Thanksgiving feast. Maybe your thing is canning and preserving the garden's bounty. Determining your objective in the veggie garden will shape what plants you grow and how much space and resources you allocate to each endeavor.

COOL SEASON VERSUS WARM SEASON VEGGIES

Cool Season......... Asparagus, Beets, Broccoli, Brussels sprouts, Cabbage, Carrots, Cauliflower, Celery, Collards, Endive, Kale, Kohlrabi, Lettuce, Mibuna, Mizuna, Mustard, Onions, Parsnips, Peas, Radicchio, Radishes, Salsify, Shallots, Spinach, Swiss chard, Tatsoi, Turnips

Warm Season...... Basil, Cantaloupe, Corn, Cucumber, Eggplant, Melons, Okra, Parsley, Peppers, Potatoes, Pumpkin, Snap beans, Soybeans, Summer squash, Sweet potatoes, Tomatillo, Tomatoes, Watermelon, Winter squash, Zucchini

△ School gardens are a great way to integrate science with the rest of the school curriculum.

△ Is there anything better than picking and eating a big juicy heirloom tomato straight from the garden?

△ You'll find it easy to can tomato juice, tomato paste, and fresh, whole tomatoes to use throughout the winter.

VEGETABLE GARDEN DESIGN TIPS

- Site the vegetable garden in full sun. (That means at least six hours or more per day.)

- Mark out the general area for your veggie garden before breaking ground, using baking flour to "draw" the lines/boundaries.

- Plan for walkways between the beds to avoid compacting the soil in the garden beds.

- Create vegetable garden beds that are about 4 feet across so that you can comfortably reach harvests from either side without setting foot into the bed.

- Study your design for a while and make sure that everything is exactly where you want it before beginning work on a new garden space. When you're satisfied with the layout, it's time to roll up your sleeves and get dirty!

Incorporating Animals

Why not add chickens, bees, and fish-farming to your organic gardening? All three benefit the garden by providing pest control, pollination, and fertilizer. Plus, you get the benefits of eggs, honey, and, if you have a *really* big tank/pond, fish to eat. (The ability to grow tomatoes and other vegetables hydroponically and organically with the help of fish is enough of a reason to incorporate aquaponics if you're feeling experimental.)

△ If you want all egg layers, buy sexed chicks so you don't end up with a rooster.

CHICKENS

There are dozens of books and resources on gardening with chickens. If you're interested in chickens, researching first is a very good idea because there are some specific requirements for successfully raising, housing, caring, and protecting them from chicks to adulthood.

You'll need to find ways to keep chickens out of any planting beds with seedlings, as they will eat young seedlings or scratch them into oblivion. Established plants are better suited for handling chicken traffic. Despite the difficulties, incorporating chickens into your garden can be highly rewarding. Besides the obvious egg production, chickens are adept at eating anything moving in the garden, especially garden pests. Just know what you're getting yourself into before bringing them home.

◁ Chicken coops protect birds from predators likely to attack at night.

▽ Chickens are excellent at controlling common garden insect pests.

BEES

Bees are another element to add to the garden and an essential one in the permaculture garden. Bees pollinate our crops and produce sweet honey; that alone should be all the reason you need. But bees are not for everyone because they require a bit of work. Again, there are many resources on the subject of beekeeping, and you should do your research before ordering a hive and queen. Consider growing gardens abundant in fall flowers if you plan to keep bees. They travel for miles looking for pollen, which is somewhat scarce during the fall. Choose composite flowers, such as zinnias, asters, Joe-pye weed, goldenrod, and perennial sunflowers, as they pack more pollen flower for flower compared to simple-flowered plants.

▷ Hobby beekeeping supports honeybee populations.

△ Honeybees are important pollinators.

△ Find a local beekeeping club and you'll have access to honey extractors, lots of beekeeping information, and like-minded individuals.

AQUACULTURE AND HYDROPONICS

Aquaculture is the practice of raising fish in large tanks, then using the nutrient-rich wastewater to fertilize plants—usually edible plants. The wastewater requires a bit of natural processing by bacteria to convert the ammonia-loaded fish waste into nitrates, but once it's treated, the wastewater is a potent source of nutrients. Tilapia are the favored freshwater fish for this system because they are easy to raise, have fast growth rates, and they're tasty! In fact, tilapia have been farmed for thousands of years.

If you're not planning to eat the fish you're growing but still want to incorporate aquaponics, there are smaller fish types available. Consult online aquaponics retailers for more information.

Hydroponics involves growing plants in water without soil. Plants are placed in grow units that anchor the plant, allowing the "aboveground" portion of the plant to emerge and thrive while the "below-ground" roots are contained inside a plastic grow chamber. Depending on the size of the system, this chamber can be PVC pipe, a plastic bucket, or a larger commercial-sized unit.

The roots are constantly bathed or misted with a nutrient/water solution that is pH adjusted for immediate plant uptake and contains all the nutrients plants need to grow and thrive. These systems can be grown in a greenhouse under the sun or indoors. If growing indoors, you must pay special attention to lighting and HVAC (heating, venting, and air-conditioning) controls to maximize production and get the best results. Hydroponics systems can also be used outdoors but special care should be taken to monitor pH and nutrient levels regularly, as an evening rainstorm can change water and nutrient levels in an outdoor hydroponic system.

△ Aquaponics can be practiced at home or in commercial operations.

△ Hydroponic systems produce bountiful yields. They're especially helpful for gardeners in areas with root knot nematode problems.

There is some debate among the NOSB and NOP regarding hydroponics over whether a "non-soil" method can truly be called organic even if it uses only organic inputs. Because taking care of the soil is one of the tenets of certified organic farms, it's argued that a non-soil method falls outside the official designation of organics. The experts will eventually make their decision on this topic, but in practice at home, the debate doesn't matter. If you grow hydroponically and use organic inputs, your harvest will still be fresh, local, and as organic as if you grew it in the soil. For those interested in hydroponics or aquaculture, there are plenty of local and online specialty hydroponic supply stores to find supplies for your garden.

△ Plant a pollinator garden, which is as beautiful as it is functional.

Mixed Borders and Beds

Mixed borders are exactly what they sound like—garden beds that include trees, shrubs, perennials, annuals, bulbs, and, if you want, edibles. The true "mixed border" style is popular in the UK but it has been embraced everywhere for its lush look in the landscape. Most planting areas we conversationally know as "flower beds" are really mixed borders.

Give thought to what you want from the bed. Privacy? Plants for pollinators and birds? Or just a beautiful garden? Start with choosing the plants that will be the largest at maturity, such as small trees or shrubs, then work your way down to the ground layer of perennials and bulbs. Don't forget to leave space for annuals or tropicals if you like the annual exuberance of these garden beauties.

If you need help choosing plants that thrive in your local zone, take a couple of trips to local mom-and-pop garden centers to check out your options. Visiting garden centers is always a fun and refreshing opportunity for garden inspiration!

When planning and planting a new garden, try to cover all available soil space, as this will reduce weed pressure and give the garden a full lush look right away. Check spacing guidelines on the tag that comes with your plant, but plant in tight-knit groups to cover the soil. If budget-strapped, buy perennials in smaller pot sizes in place of larger ones. Small plants grow up fairly quickly, and will fill in the bed space. Go with larger plants for the specimens, such as shrubs or small trees.

◁ Mixed borders of shrubs, trees, annuals, perennials, bulbs, and even edibles have fewer pest problems than monocultures.

INSTALLING A MIXED BORDER

The basics of planting and garden bed-building are fairly similar from garden type to garden type. Here's what you need to know in order to build a diverse and unique organic garden.

Building new garden beds. Many of these initial installation techniques are the same whether you're preapring a vegetable garden, a bed for cut flowers, or a planting hole for a tree. The best time to create new beds is generally in early spring after the ground thaws and when the weather starts to warm up or in late fall after the heat of the summer is past.

- Remove all vegetation from the area to start. If there are weeds or larger plants, try weed whacking or mowing down the plants to ground level.

- Physically dig out the remaining stems and roots. It's important to get the roots, as many plants can shoot right back up if their root system is left in place. It's the same concept when weeding: you have to get the roots!

- Use a shovel or digging fork if going manual. You can also rent specialized equipment, such as a turf or sod cutter to physically remove the vegetation.

- Rake over the area in a final pass to remove loose bits of weeds and dug-up roots. You are now ready to add compost.

- Add a 2-inch layer of compost to the entire bed. Mix compost into the soil by digging one shovel depth down to turn over the soil, or use a tiller to blend the compost into the soil.

❧ TURNING OVER THE SOIL

The term "turn over the soil" is used all the time but rarely is the process actually described. Here is how it is done:

1. Plunge your shovel into soil down to the hilt, using your weight to press down on the top of the shovel blade with your foot.

2. Lever back on the handle to free up a shovel's worth of soil from the surrounding ground.

3. Rotate the shovel over 180 degrees to flip over the load of soil, landing it in the same spot from which it was removed.

4. Give that turned shovelful of soil a chop or two with your shovel to break it up slightly into approximately equal size pieces. Even though you're breaking it up slightly, it should stay chunky. Resist the urge to break it down to little pieces, as this reduces soil porosity and can lead to many problems down the road.

5. Continue this process until the entire bed has been turned over.

- Remove any rocks that come to the surface and save them for a future project. I use rocks to line beds or circle newly planted trees.

- Rake the bed smooth once you've incorporated the compost and turned over the bed to prepare for planting. It doesn't have to be perfect, but try for a mostly smooth bed. This will help even out seed germination when sowing seed directly into the bed.

Double digging. This method involves removing one shovel depth of soil and placing it to the side, then doing the soil-turning procedure described to the left on the lower layer of soil—including adding a 2-inch compost layer before starting the process of turning over the lower layer of soil. Once complete with the lower layer, put the soil you placed aside back on the bed, add another 2-inch layer of compost, and follow the same instructions to break up big chunks slightly.

△ Leave the soil chunky when turning it over.

△ Pine or cedar boards are the most common type of wood used in raised bed construction.

△ For a more rustic look, build raised beds with old tree logs. As a bonus, logs may last longer than cut lumber.

△ Raised beds give the gardener more control over the soil structure and texture.

Raised Bed Gardens

Gardening in raised beds is an alternative to digging directly into your native garden soil. Raised beds are beneficial if you have concerns about potential soil contamination, such as near older homes where the soil may contain lead paint chips or dust which may be taken up by edible plants.

Raised beds also are a good idea whenever the existing native soil is of poor quality. When homes are constructed, the fill soil used around the yard and foundation may be of rather poor quality, with just a thin layer of topsoil spread on top in order to grow turf grass. Genuine gardening can be difficult in this soil, so a raised bed in which you can create your own garden soil is a perfect solution.

△ Use your imagination when building raised beds. Just don't make the beds wider than 4 feet or it will be difficult to reach the plants in order to tend to them from the edge of the bed.

Raised beds also are easier on your back because they reduce the amount of bending over required to work in the garden. They are perfect for people with physical limitations. They also don't require much in the way of digging and tilling to get started, though they still require some physical labor to install. Well-crafted raised beds also provide an edge to sit on when gardening or relaxing in the garden. Remember, don't sit on the soil!

Tips for Raised Bed Gardening

- Material choice impacts how long the garden lasts. Pine breaks down faster than cedar. Raw-cut tree logs or branches are great because they add to soil health as they break down slowly over time.

- Don't use pressure-treated wood. If you must, put plastic between the soil and pressure-treated wood to keep chemicals from leaching into garden beds.

- Build raised beds that are at least 6 inches tall so that there's plenty of soil for growing root crops. A depth of 8 to 12 inches is even better!

- Get creative! Raised beds are a reflection of your personality and taste.

- Build raised beds with a mixture of topsoil and a blend of composts. A blend of 50-percent topsoil and a 50-percent compost mixture is ideal. For even richer beds, go with a 25-percent topsoil and 75-percent compost blend.

Maintenance

Maintenance is a word that conjures up thoughts of sweat, hard work, chores, and drudgery. But maintaining a garden is anything but a chore when viewed with the right perspective. In addition to the obvious health benefits of working in the fresh air, maintaining the garden gives the gardener time to pause and reflect on the past year's garden growth. Did the flower display go as you planned? Did you plant enough of a particular type of vegetable? Did you miss out on seeing a particular type of butterfly larvae in your garden by not planting their preferred host plant? The best time to think about the garden is while you're *in* the garden. For most gardeners, the routine maintenance tasks quickly take on a meditative joy.

Plus, research proves that being out in nature benefits humans in many ways. Think of it as a free workout that comes with a suite of health benefits and a sense of accomplishment at the end of the day.

FALL AND WINTER MAINTENANCE

There are a few key maintenance tasks to complete each season in the garden. Fall has us removing leaves from our lawns and saving them for composting. Rake or blow them into a pile right next to your composter for layering convenience, or chop and bag them with your lawnmower and add them to your composter. If you don't have enough space on your property to compost, bag them up for the local municipality to compost.

Some people remove the previous season's growth in the fall, clearing their garden beds of all plant debris. However, late winter is a better time to clean up garden beds. Leaving perennial stems in your garden beds encourages beneficial insects to overwinter in your garden. Insects need places to hide from winter's cold and any remaining seedheads are food for birds during the harsh winter months. Don't forget to look out for praying mantis egg sacks when cleaning out the garden!

△ Toward the end of summer, hot and humid weather encourages growth of powdery mildew. Always discard affected plants at the end of the season. Do not compost them.

One exception would be plants affected by disease. Any diseased plant material should be removed in the fall, as you don't want the disease to spread in your garden.

The vegetable garden should also be cleaned to the ground each year to remove any sources of garden pests, diseases, or insects. We don't need pests overwintering in our veggie gardens! You don't have to remove every single leaf that fell to the ground, but try to remove as much as possible to reduce potential impact on next year's crops. Put garden debris in the compost pile if it's not diseased, or send it off to be composted by your local municipality if disease is present.

After veggie beds are clear of debris, add a 2-inch layer of compost to build soil fertility. The compost protects garden soil over winter and once spring rolls in, you can dig the compost into the beds when planting spring veggies.

WEEDING

Take the time to weed correctly, which means digging out the roots. If you pull out only leaves, you're missing the roots, which means you will have to weed again and again as the roots resprout. Use a tool designed for weeding to make the job easy. The Japanese tool called a hori-hori knife makes a great weeder. Undercut hoes are designed for quick weeding between crop rows or plants. There is also a weeding tool called a CobraHead that makes short work of weeds.

All these tools are available at your local garden center, and when properly maintained, these types of tools cut through soil like butter to strike fear into the heart of any weed. Keep them clean, and periodically sharpen them with a file, whetstone, or bench grinder. Weeds that have not yet gone to seed can be composted, but unless you are confident that your composter gets hot enough to kill seeds, weeds with seedheads on them should be sent to the municipal compost.

▽ Compost weeds that haven't gone to seed.

△ Bypass pruners are essential tools for every gardener.

△ Pruning saws cut on the upstroke.

△ Loppers allow for cutting of larger branches.

△ Proper pruning ensures longevity of trees by limiting weather damage.

PRUNING

The best time of year to prune plants depends on the species you're pruning. Most are best pruned in late winter before growth resumes in spring. However, some spring-flowering plants only bloom on the previous season's growth. For plants with this characteristic, the best time to prune is just after flowering in spring. Make sure to disinfect your pruners at least once a year. Dipping blades in household rubbing alcohol (buy the 91 percent type, not the 70 percent) for 60 seconds will disinfect the blade and kill any pathogens.

Always use sharp tools made for the size of limb you're pruning, and wear personal protective equipment when necessary. A good pair of hand pruners for smaller branches, a good pair of loppers for larger branches, and a pruning saw for small limbs should be in every gardener's tool shed. Chainsaws are the next step up, but for many, hiring a professional is the way to go when chainsaws are required. Unless it's a mature tree that needs pruning, the smaller tools are all you'll ever need.

Why Prune?

Pruning is done to remove dead wood, to improve the structural integrity of the plant, or to guide future growth. Remove dead wood to reduce the possibility it will injure someone or something, should the dead wood fall. Trees are pruned for structural integrity to remove branches that cross each other, as crossing branches rub against each other and weaken these contact points, which can also cause hazards to people. Eventually, crossing branches can cause damage leading to disease or insect infestation.

Trees are also pruned to guide future growth. This type of pruning shapes the tree's final habit and structure. All trees need a good leader branch, as the leader branch is the top of any tree and grows the fastest each year. If a tree splits into two leaders, choose the healthiest one and remove the other with a clean and sharp pair of pruners. Remove the weaker one by pruning back to the base of the healthy leader branch.

As an organic gardener devoted to natural practices, you should take a plant's true form and final size into account when planning your garden. Avoid shearing plants back into the "meatball" shapes that were once standard practice for foundation plantings. Seeing plants achieve their true form and natural growth habit is a joy to behold and it reduces maintenance work. There are people who get a kind of Zen-like pleasure from pruning shrubs each year, but such an aesthetic may not be appropriate for the true organic gardener because it is potentially injurious to many plants. If this is a serious hobby for you, you might select an evergreen shrub or two that you can prune to your heart's content for holiday arrangements, and spare the rest of your plants.

◁ Tree topping leads to weak and unattractive growth.

❧ DON'T TOP YOUR TREES!

You may have seen trees that have been "topped." Topped trees are chopped back without regard to stem size or concern about maintaining healthy growth of the remaining branches. Topping trees is not a correct pruning method and it can very seriously injure healthy trees. If any contractor ever suggests topping your trees, send them packing and seek a contractor who actually understands how trees grow and how they should be pruned.

Dividing Perennials

Dividing perennials is another common and necessary task in the garden. Dividing plants increases their vitality, allows you to remove weak or damaged growth, and gives you more plants to share with friends or plant elsewhere in your garden.

Some perennials need this process every few years to stay healthy. If a perennial looks like it hasn't grown very much in a couple years, that may be a sign it needs to be divided. There certainly are perennials that do not need to be divided to thrive, so if you are looking for less maintenance in your garden, seek out those plants. Plants that grow by underground runners are one such type. They keep marching forward, leaving older roots behind. Plants that grow in basal clumps are more likely to need division every few years to stay healthy.

Ultimately, a garden is an extension of your life interests and your unique aesthetic taste. Time spent planning out garden spaces on your property is time well spent. Think cohesively and plan for sustainability to reduce maintenance and conserve resources. Garden maintenance need not be a chore, as it gives time to pause and reflect on lessons learned in this year's garden. Keep up on maintenance tasks to sustain and encourage healthy plant growth.

▽ Dividing perennials can stimulate new growth and blooms, as well as give you more (free) plants.

10

Organic Container Gardens

So far, we've learned that organic gardening involves taking care of the soil. But if the soil is in a container and not in the ground, can it still be considered organic? The short answer is yes. If you purchase OMRI-listed potting soil for the containers, the plants can be considered to have been grown organically, as long as you follow organic growing methods. It's a bit more complicated when you talk about certified organic farms because a central tenet of organic farming is soil care, involving crop rotation, fallow periods, cover cropping, and other methodologies, none of which are used when gardening in containers. But while the USDA may debate the definition of certified organic around this topic, in the backyard you can certainly follow practices that ensure your container garden is 100 percent organic.

◁ Organic container gardens are all about the inputs.

△ Try to source organically grown plants for container gardens. However, you can also purchase conventionally grown plants and maintain them organically when you bring them home.

△ Container gardens make decks and patios more aesthetically pleasing.

△ Growing edibles on porches and patios puts them close to the site of consumption. Just don't pick and eat everything before dinner!

Container gardening has gained momentum over the years for good reason. Containers do not require heavy digging, so are easier for people with physical limitations to plant and maintain. They can be changed out quickly, allowing gardeners to go from summer containers to fall containers in an afternoon. For apartment dwellers with limited access to a small porch, container gardens may be the only option to enjoy the fruits of nature. Container gardens can be completed in much less time as compared to traditional garden beds, they require less maintenance, and they provide immediate gratification once complete. Generally, container gardens are placed closer to the home and beautify the landscape in hardscaped areas such as a deck or patio.

Container gardens are great for gardeners that haven't quite put down roots, or those who are renting and haven't yet purchased their own home. Growing in containers allows you to sharpen your gardening skills and still take your garden treasures with you when you relocate.

Additionally, gardening in containers allows you to move plants on a whim, no digging required. If you want to see how a particular combination looks together, you can move them around in an afternoon. Container gardening also allows you the benefit of moving plants immediately if you discover you placed them in too much or too little sun: you can rectify the situation in a few minutes by situating them in areas better suited to their individual needs. My favorite container garden relocation is to move a rather fragrant blooming plant close to my sitting areas on my porch, patio, or deck. Weekend moments on the porch with coffee or tea and a pleasantly sweet-smelling plant close-by? Nirvana!

Here's how to grow your own gorgeous organic container gardens.

Selecting the Right Type of Container

Most container gardens are planted in plastic or terracotta (pots made from orange-colored, unglazed ceramic clay) containers. Either can be obtained from local garden shops. Plastic containers are more economical to purchase and hold moisture better than terracotta, which is porous and "breathes" more than solid plastic. Although terracotta pots require more frequent watering, one advantage is that the pots allow for faster wet and dry cycles in the potting soil, which helps spur growth rates.

Consider using a glazed ceramic pot if you want the container to hold more moisture. This is a good "in between" choice. There are thousands of types of ceramic glazed containers in every color of the rainbow to suit individual tastes, but all will crack if the soil inside them freezes solid. It's best to empty ceramic or terracotta containers of soil and store them upside-down for the winter if you want to guarantee their use the following season (unless you live in a subtropical climate, in which case you can ignore that piece of advice and garden year-round).

Fiber pots such as Smart Pots® or Root Pouch® are relative newcomers to the world of gardening containers. They combine the utility and light weight of plastic pots with the breathability of terracotta. Fiber pots come in all sizes and colors and some even come with handles. These pots last many seasons, are not subject to breaking if the soil inside them freezes, and they can be sterilized in between crops if desired. And it's easy to remove old rootballs from fiber pots. Run your hand around the rootball, just inside the pot. Just like pulling up on a Velcro strip, the rootball will become detached from the fiber pot for easy removal.

Window boxes and hanging baskets are two classic examples of planting containers. Window boxes are more popular in urban environments where outdoor gardening opportunities are scarce. There are even containers designed with a window box look, but which are made to attach to railings on a deck or porch. Hanging baskets are everywhere in summer, and are readily available in pre-designed and pre-planted form at your local garden center.

△ Fiber pots are reusable, but can dry out quickly. Take care to water frequently during the summer in hot locations.

△ Window boxes are making a comeback, particularly for urban gardeners.

△ Almost anything can be a container.

△ Check architectural salvage shops for unusual containers.

△ Insert a little whimsy into your garden!

Even though most container gardens are planted in traditional pots, any container that holds soil can work. Anything can be transformed into a container garden if it can hold enough soil to plant something: whiskey barrels cut in half, broken ceramic cups, old shoes or boots, tires, old dressers, old filing cabinets, 50-gallon drums . . . the list could go on forever, and is only limited by your creativity. Ideally, the container choice will allow for a sufficient volume of soil to support the plants chosen to grow in it. Basic translation: If you have a broken coffee cup, try planting one succulent in it, not a tomato plant. Bigger containers hold more soil and can therefore hold more plants or larger plants.

CONTAINERS SAFE FOR EDIBLES

If using a recycled unconventional container, such as a tire, to grow edibles, remember to clean it sufficiently so you are not contaminating the garden soil. Better yet, use containers that might be contaminated to grow ornamental plants, and save the edibles for plastic or terracotta containers, or grow them in larger raised-bed type containers made from wood or concrete block.

▷ Old tires are very hard to recycle, so if you have a few, you can use them as small "raised bed" containers for small trailing plants, with taller plants near the center.

Designing the Container Garden

When selecting plants for a container garden, gather the plants together on a cart at the local garden center so you can see what they look like clumped together. Before buying, mix and match plants to arrive at arrangements you like.

Don't be afraid to jam lots of plants together in the pot. If they fit inside the confines of the pot diameter, the arrangement will work. Keep in mind, though, the more plants you jam into a container, the more often you'll have to water. Young plants will also grow up and expand, so make sure and leave some room for them to reach their full potential. If in doubt, ask a garden center employee how big your plant choices will get. If shopping in late spring, odds are the plants will already be grown up enough to get a good sense of their late-season size. You can always pull the plants apart at the end of the season and repot/repurpose them into other containers.

△ When planting a large container, also use large plants so everything is to scale.

The best container designs have a variety of sizes, colors, and textures in them. When designing your container garden, you get to choose the details. Maybe you want all white flowers, or maybe you want all texture and no flowers, but there are no bad decisions because you are designing what makes you happy. Here are a few pointers for creating killer container garden combinations.

△ Take plants for a "test drive" at the garden center.

△ A traditional "thriller, spiller, filler" container.

THRILLERS, SPILLERS, AND FILLERS

Traditional container design theory says for maximum impact you should have the classic elements: thrillers, spillers, and fillers. One plant is chosen to be the center of attention, or the thriller. Spillers are plants that literally spill over the sides of the container and cascade down toward the ground. The fillers are there to add color or texture, completing the container by filling in around the thriller and spiller elements.

Thriller plants demand attention and really make people notice your container. I like to use larger plants for this design element, such as a woody plant or something tropical, but you can also use non-plant elements as the thriller, such as bamboo poles spray-painted a bright color, a repurposed piece of wrought-iron garden art, or any other favorite item that might serve as the starring element in your container. There is a "golden rule" in container design that says that the thriller should be approximately two times the height of your container for maximum impact. So if you have a two-foot-tall pot, your thriller should extend four feet above the top of the container.

Spillers cascade down the sides of the container and provide the base element of interest. The best containers will look like there is a waterfall of plants gushing over the edge and splashing toward the ground. Spillers are planted at the pot's edge so

△ 'Dragon's Breath'™ celosia is a perfect thriller.

△ Calibrachoa (top) and Diamond Frost® euphorbia (bottom)

THRILLERS

Abutilon

Eucalyptus

Found objects

Gaura

Nicotiana

Ornamental grasses

Papyrus

Tropical plants

Woody plants

Yucca

SPILLERS

Angel wing begonia

Bacopa

Ipomea

Lantana

Lotus

Lysimachia

Portulaca

Scaevola

Thyme

Verbena

FILLERS

Ageratum

Cuphea

Ferns

Geranium

Gomphrena

Nemesia

Osteospermum

Pentas

Salvia

Zinnia

they can get started growing over the sides immediately. Spillers also soften the edges of a pot and help make the entire container just look huggable.

Fillers are the supporting cast and are used to accentuate the rest of the container choices. They literally fill the space between the top of the pot and the lower edge of the thriller design element. Fillers should not take away from the thriller, but help it shine. Consider a variety of sizes when choosing fillers so you have multiple layers of interest in the container. Choosing one plant variety that is one-third the size of the thriller and one that is two-thirds the size of the thriller adds even more variety.

Making these choices is fun and rewarding. As the container grows in over the course of a season, you can always edit as needed to keep the container looking its best. Fillers growing too fast and overtaking your thriller? Just snip them back a bit to reduce their size. Fast-growing spillers overtaking your fillers? Either snip them back or move their trailing growth to a different part of the container that hasn't filled in as fast. Have you packed too many plants into the container? Surgically remove one or two of the fillers by carefully digging them out, then adjust the remaining foliage to make it look like nothing ever happened. Plant the extracted fillers in a different container or elsewhere in the garden.

△ Placing large containers on feet or wheels helps protect the surface upon which the plant rests.

Planting the Container Garden

Just as following the proper planting technique is important to ensure the health of in-ground plants, so it goes with container garden plants.

CONSIDER CONTAINER WEIGHT

When considering container options, don't forget the weight factor. Ceramic containers are much heavier than plastic, and once they are filled with soil they are even heavier. If potting large ceramic containers, place them empty in their final location before adding potting soil. One way to make containers lighter is to reduce the amount of soil added. For containers larger than 24 inches tall, you can place something in the bottom of the container to reduce the amount of soil needed. There are products specifically designed for this purpose, such as pot inserts that come in a variety of sizes. Even a 2- to 3-inch reduction in the amount of soil in the bottom of the pot will help reduce weight.

There are also planter movers that, like appliance movers, have straps that "hug" the pot and allow you to safely move it. The straps go over your shoulders and allow you to lift the pot with your legs and not your back. Always test the lift before putting the full weight of a pot on yourself, and ask a friend for help. If in doubt, leave the pot where it is until the season is over, then remove the soil before moving the pot to a new location.

You can also buy a base with locking wheels and place the container on it before filling with soil. Wheels allow you to move the container around easily. Don't forget to lock the wheels back in place when you're done moving so it doesn't run away. Wheeled bases also keep the pot off the deck or patio, which helps reduce the incidence of "pot stains" that inevitably occur when any container sits long enough on a deck or patio surface. These pot stains can be scrubbed or pressure-washed off a deck easily, but the staining can also be reduced by using "pot feet." There are many different manufacturers of pot feet, but they all function the same way, by elevating the pot slightly off the deck surface to minimize any staining. All potting soils have a tendency to stain slightly, as they are made from organic matter that is constantly breaking down.

SELECT THE RIGHT POTTING SOIL

Container gardens require potting soil, which is not the same as garden soil. Remember, garden soil consists of sand, silt, and clay. Potting soil, on the other hand, is actually a soilless mix with specific properties formulated to perform well in container gardens.

Containers do not thrive if you dig up soil from the backyard to use as your container soil. Not only will this soil have less air space, but it could also transfer pests or diseases into your container gardens. Look for potting soils made for outdoor use when shopping for your outdoor container gardens. Outdoor, all-purpose potting soils such as Organic Mechanics® Container Blend are designed to provide good drainage to avoid over-saturated containers. Indoor houseplant potting soils are designed to hold water a bit longer than outdoor soils, because indoor houseplants generally go much longer between watering. Comparatively, outdoor containers dry out faster and need to be watered several times per week during the growing season.

One of the drawbacks of a container garden is that they are less forgiving than gardens in the ground. This means that if you forget to water for a few days, your container gardens could dry up and be quite crispy by the time you get around to watering them. Fortunately, in most cases their beauty and joy outweigh the work of frequent watering.

To combat the frequent need for water, container gardens can be planted with potting soils that are formulated to hold moisture. Look for potting soils that contain ingredients with superior moisture-holding abilities, including compost, worm castings, and coconut husk fiber. Check potting soil labels closely, as some products have chemical polymer crystals added to absorb water, which are not organic.

What about adding gravel and pot shards? Some people swear by adding gravel or stone to the bottom of big, ornamental pots to increase drainage. Not only does this make the pots even heavier, but it also does not improve drainage. The soil above the gravel layer holds moisture longer than if there were no layer of gravel. By adding two distinct layers of materials—the layer of gravel and layer of soil—you create what is known as a perched water table and the upper soil layer must completely saturate before any drainage can occur from the soil layer down through the gravel layer. Plastic pots generally have enough drain holes in the bottom of the container to allow for good drainage.

Garden long enough and you'll accumulate many broken terracotta pots. These can be broken into shards that can be placed in the bottom of a container. Place one shard directly over the drain hole if planting in a new terracotta container (there is usually only one drain hole in terracotta containers). Ideally, the shard should curve over the drain hole to keep soil from blocking it and clogging up the drain hole. Place a couple others around it to make sure soil doesn't block things up. Larger pot shards work best.

HOW TO PLANT A CONTAINER GARDEN

1. Select your container. Make sure it's clean and free of any debris.

2. Assemble your plants for the container. Make sure the plants are watered well and not dry. Note which plant is in the largest-sized pot and how large that pot is, as this impacts the next step.

3. Add enough soil to fill the container to the level where you can drop in your largest rootball so that the top of the rootball will be about ¼- to ½-inch below the top of the pot.

△ Check container gardens frequently to make sure they stay watered.

4. Remove that largest plant from the pot, and place it in the container. Add soil around the base of the plant's rootball just so the plant does not fall over.

5. Repeat the process of adding soil until you have enough placed to support the filler plants and keep all the rootballs at the same height (about ¼- to ½-inch below the top of the pot).

6. Place the filler plants. Once they're added, fill in any gaps with soil so there are no empty pockets of air in-between plants.

7. Add your spillers at the pot edges, making sure to line up the rootballs so they are at the same height as the rest of the plants.

8. Fill in any remaining gaps with soil so the soil line is the same height across the entire container. Pay special attention to the edges to make sure soil surrounds the rootball of every plant.

9. Pick up the planter about ½-inch off the ground, then drop it (gently) to the ground after all plants are in place. This helps settle the soil into place and improve soil to rootball contact.

10. Move the container to the spot where it will live. *Then* water it well. If you water in before moving it, you just make the container heavier.

Caring for a Container Garden

Prevent pest problems and grow big beautiful container gardens by giving them the best care.

WATER

The easiest way to check whether your plants need water is by using your finger to test for moisture. Stick a finger into the soil. If you only get one knuckle deep and feel moisture, you can wait to water. If you get two knuckles deep and still don't feel moisture, it's time to water. Make sure to fill in where you poked the soil.

When rechecking in a day or two, check in a different spot. Soon you'll get a feel for how often to water, though this can change based on weather or environmental conditions. Hotter weather or sun exposure means more frequent watering is needed.

You can also test the moisture content of a pot by lifting it from the pot edge. Heavier pots contain more water. Lighter pots will tip easily when lifted without too much effort. It's a quick trick that's not quite as accurate, but with experience you'll soon learn how to know if the pot needs water by weight.

FERTILIZE

We've talked about soil and water, but fertilizer is the last essential element for successful, exuberant containers. All plants need fertilizer to grow and container gardens are no exception. Container gardens are an enclosed system, which means that everything the plant roots need to grow will have to be already inside the container or added as fertilizer.

The easiest way to fertilize containers is to add a measured dose of an all-purpose fertilizer at planting time. If planting flowering plants, look for fertilizers with a high phosphorus number (the middle number in the three-number sequence; in a 4-6-4 fertilizer, the 6 represents the phosphorus ratio). If the plants are all foliage, then nitrogen (the first number in the three-number sequence) is the most important. Follow the instructions on the label when determining how often to reapply fertilizer throughout the season for best results and optimum growth. Make sure to use organic fertilizers!

TROUBLESHOOTING

Help! There are mushrooms growing out of my containers!

Relax. Potting soil is made of organic material, and fungi eat organic material. Under some circumstances, you may see mushrooms growing out of even an indoor container. Don't fret, as mushrooms are part of a natural organic soil and garden. However, if they bother you, start by removing the mushrooms as soon as they are visible.

To prevent future outbreaks, take the plant outside and remove the rootball from the pot. Gently remove as much soil as possible, taking care not to damage the roots too much. Plants are tough and can handle a little root loss during a repot. Discard all the removed soil in a garden bed. After this is done, give the roots a little soak in a fresh container full of water (mix in a little liquid kelp or some worm castings for an extra boost). A 10- to 15-minute soak is all you need. Then repot in a new pot with fresh potting soil. Save the old pot and let it sit outside for a bit to air out and get washed by rain. You can use the old pot again after it has been outside for a couple of weeks.

Although rare, this mushroom problem also happens with outdoor containers from time to time. Outside, the plants can be left alone: the mushrooms will run their course and recede after a week or two. The presence of mushrooms is actually a good thing, as it indicates your potting soil is being broken down into plant-available nutrients by the fungi that spawned the mushrooms. If the mushrooms bother you, though, simply remove and compost them. If they come back and you feel you must remove them, follow the process described above to replace all the potting soil in the container and around the rootball.

Yearly Maintenance

Do you need to replace the potting soil every year? That depends. Some potting soils are more reusable than others. Potting soil for outdoor containers should automatically be discarded if plants grown in it died due to plant diseases. If the potting soil grew beautiful plants all season and the plants only died because winter's frost arrived, then you can reuse the entire container of potting soil the following season.

Potting soils made with compost and aged pine bark last longer than peat-based potting soils, as compost and aged pine bark have already undergone a managed decomposition process and are more resistant to breaking down. If you need to remove the soil to protect a ceramic pot, you can place the soil in plastic bags for the winter. Leave the bags open so the soil can breathe. Place the potting soil back in the container when night temperatures are consistently above freezing (above 32°F).

Growing Indoor Houseplants Organically

Don't forget to take care of your houseplants! You can grow houseplants organically, just as you'd grow outdoor container gardens, though it takes a few adaptations, as described below.

LIGHT

Most houseplants will thrive in bright indoor light but take care when placing houseplants in full sun. Houseplants generally thrive in low-light conditions present inside the home, as most houseplants are species that occupy the forest understory in nature. This means they can thrive in lower light levels typical of indoor conditions.

Resist the urge to place houseplants outside in summertime as direct sun can cause sunburn on leaves. If you are intent on placing plants outside, you can slowly acclimate them to higher light conditions. Start them out in a shady area for a week or two so they can begin the acclimatization process. Gradually move them into more and more light over the course of a couple weeks. If leaves start to show signs of burn, move them back into shadier conditions. Burned leaves will look washed out and turn yellow or white before dying back.

WATER

Be aware of plant placement inside your home, as plants close to a source of radiant heat will dry out faster than plants farther from heat sources. If your home is consistently dry from winter heating, this will also dry out soils faster. Using the same knuckle test described for outdoor container gardens, check frequently to see if your plants need water. After a few months of doing this, you'll know about how often to water each houseplant. Monitor your plants, and water as soon as soils dry out. If plants are in cooler conditions during fall and winter, they will use less water and therefore do not need as much water as they require during spring or summer.

Timing for watering can even vary in different locations in the house, due to the unique microclimates present in different rooms. Keeping tabs on your plants will help ensure they don't sit dry for too long and are not overwatered. The number one cause of plant death is loving them too much and watering too frequently!

REPOTTING

Periodically, houseplants need repotting. When plants stop growing, if leaves are yellowing, or if roots are circling at the bottom of the container, it's time to repot.

Take the plant outside because repotting is messy. Pull the plant out of the pot and take a look at the roots. If they are spindly and the rootball falls apart a bit when you pulled it out of the pot, place it back in the pot, replacing any lost soil as necessary, then add a low-dose organic fertilizer (such as worm castings), and return it to its spot in your home. Sometimes plants simply need a fertilizer shot rather than repotting to start growing again. Worm castings are great to invigorate a houseplant. Also, they smell earthy like soil, which is much more pleasant than stronger and smellier fertilizers, such as fish emulsion.

If roots look healthy and have filled the inside of the pot, it's time to repot in a container the next size up. This means choosing a pot that is only a few inches wider than the current one. Place enough organic soil in the bottom of the container to accommodate the rootball. To test the depth, place the rootball on the soil you put in the new pot. The top of the rootball should line up approximately ¼- to ½-inch below the top of the new pot, which allows enough room for watering.

Then add a little soil at a time around the sides, making sure you keep the plant rootball centered so it doesn't end up lopsided when you finish. Place a handful of soil inside the pot, next to the rootball, then spread it out around the roots' outer edges. Repeat until the sides have been filled. Don't place too much pressure on the soil, as compaction reduces the pore space for air and water. Just slight pressure around the edge helps secure the soil and plant in place. You can also use water to slightly compact the soil around the edges but that can get messy. If you don't apply slight pressure to the soil as you add it around the edges, odds are that eventually you'll see the edges are lower than the rootball. In such case, you'll need to go back and add more soil. The soil around the edges and the plant's rootball should be at the same height after watering.

Indoor containers should have saucers placed beneath them to catch excess water that drains from them. Ideally, you'll add just enough water to saturate the container but not enough to overflow the saucer. Saucers under each indoor container will protect your home from spills and pot stains.

11

You *CAN* Have a Lawn . . . Organically

There are those people deeply devoted to a strict organic lifestyle for whom the mere idea of a lawn elicits derision or even hostility. And this is somewhat understandable, as the traditional method for nurturing a lawn with loads of chemical fertilizers and huge consumption of water is about as unnatural as it gets. But eliminating the lawn altogether is neither practical nor desirable for many people. In most of the country, just digging up the lawn and replacing it with something else is not feasible or sometimes even legal. In areas that receive little rainfall, that might well be the best option, but for the rest of us, living with HOA requirements or paying bills each month with little money left over for landscaping, digging up the entire lawn is a no-go. And there are also the aesthetics involved. At least some areas of broad swaths of green can be a wonderful backdrop for mixed border gardens that isn't easy to abandon.

◁ Your lawn is a gatekeeper for rainwater returning to the groundwater supply. Organically grown lawns are free from chemicals that would otherwise leach into the water system.

The good news is that *yes*, you can have a traditional lawn and grow it organically. You can also have a non-traditional lawn and grow it organically. How we manage the lawn can make a huge impact on the environment surrounding our houses. Ditching the chemicals and going organic is a good start. First, though, a little morale building for those of you with guilt over your fondness for lawns.

Why Bother with a Lawn?

First off, a lawn (or some kind of plant-cover growing where the lawn would typically be) is environmentally preferable to a flat sheet of concrete. Pavement surfaces can be between 50 to 90 degrees (F) hotter than shaded or moist surfaces. Simply having more plants around helps prevent the formation of, and mitigates impacts from, heat islands such as concrete slabs. Simply put, it's more comfortable for humans and animals to surround themselves with plants, including turf lawns and other groundcovers.

In some areas, it is lawn grass that captures most of the falling precipitation and returns it to the groundwater supply. Lawns also filter rainwater and some storm-water runoff. A paved surface inhibits both of those processes. You have perhaps noticed how, in a heavy rainstorm, water wastefully runs off parking lots and driveways into storm sewers rather than being absorbed by the ground.

In many neighborhoods, a lawn is required by homeowner's associations. If you dislike traditional turf grass lawns, avoid neighborhoods with those requirements. Unless a neighborhood covenant details the species you're required to grow, you may have choices in what types of plants with which you cover your lawns spaces. This is good news for you if you plan to transition your lawn to organic maintenance.

Even if a lawn isn't required, there's quite a bit of recreation that takes place on turf. If you have children (even more of a reason to go organic), having a space where they can kick around a ball, do flips, run, play tag, and stargaze is ideal. An organic lawn also benefits dogs and other pets, keeping their little paws free and clear from pesticide residue.

Lastly, a lawn is kind of like the frame on a picture. It gives the eye a visual break from the busy-ness of landscape beds and architecture.

So there are reasons to have a lawn, and if those apply to your situation, there are also ways to make lawn care less destructive to the environment, including for the people and animals living in it and on it.

Assessing the Situation

While it would be ideal to just tear out an old lawn and install a brand-spanking-new organic lawn that's a mixture of clover and grass seed (where that works) and moving forward with nothing but organic inputs, that's not always an option. Some turf grasses are much higher maintenance than others, so there will be some

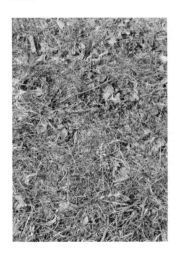

Golf courses are the classic example of non-organic turf lawn surfaces. They require enormous quantities of synthetic fertilizers and herbicides to look this way. It may be attractive to some, but is almost repulsive to organic enthusiasts. Some more progressive courses, however, have begun practicing organic and natural grounds keeping.

cases in which starting over might be the best option, but such dramatic solutions are usually not necessary. You may find, however, that you have to adjust your expectations.

The advice that follows is aimed at people who choose to work with what they have rather than start from scratch, as this is the situation that applies to most.

Before you decide what to do, take a look at where you're starting and what your goals are. Your lawn is going to be somewhere on a scale that ranges from, "It's green, mow it," to "golf course-worthy turf."

If your aspirations are simply for "it's green—mow it," you probably don't need to do anything much differently, unless the lawn isn't meeting your needs. Golf course–worthy turf, on the other hand, will require frequent, less environmentally friendly inputs, and creating and maintaining such a lawn organically will require the biggest paradigm shift.

All the maintenance and management advice of this chapter leads toward growing a lawn somewhere in the middle of the scale: nice to look at, handles the amount of foot traffic it receives, and relatively trouble-free.

Patchy spots can be indicative of a fungal problem or of the need to change grass species in the lawn.

DO I NEED TO START OVER?

Most people will be able to make do with the lawn they have and simply transition the care to a less impactful set of strategies. Others, though, will need to think about switching to a different type of grass. Here are some issues that can often be resolved with a different turf blend:

Problem   *Patchy spots where foot traffic is high.*
Solution   Switch to a turf blend that handles higher foot traffic.

Problem	*Thin turf in the shade.*
Solution	Switch to a turf that needs less light or switch to groundcovers with lower light requirements.
Problem	*Lawn grass invades neighboring landscape beds.*
Solution	Switch to a clumping grass that does not spread via rhizomes. This is possible, even in the South!
Problem	*You have to mow twice a week, otherwise the lawn looks ratty.*
Solution	Switch to a grass type that doesn't bloom quickly. Bahia, for example, is a common, low-input, warm-season turf that requires frequent mowing because of the flower heads.
Problem	*You don't want grass at all.*
Solution	Plant low-growing lawn alternatives instead.

Other problems, including bald spots, insect problems, nutrient deficiencies, and weed competition, require solutions other than a turf-species switch.

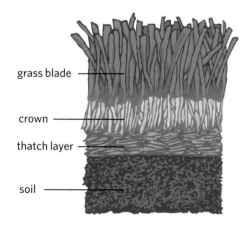

grass blade

crown

thatch layer

soil

△ These are the layers of the lawn.

Anatomy of a Lawn

It's important to understand the parts of the lawn and their relationship to one another in order to give your lawn excellent care. A lawn is more than just grass. White clover was once a popular plant for cool season lawns, and in fact, most lawns were a blend of clover and turf grass. Clover naturally fixes nitrogen, which the turf happily takes in through its roots. Growing clover also improves a lawn's resistance to drought. If you live in a cooler area, investigate overseeding the lawn with white clover to reap its many benefits.

Grass leaves. The top part of the grass is what you mow.

Grass plant crown. The place where the stems or top of the grass plant meet the roots of the grass plants is the point from which grass plants spread.

Thatch. This is an accumulated layer of dead and living stems and other organic matter between the green leaves of the grass and the soil. Leaf clippings are usually not part of the thatch layer because they break down quickly, and are incorporated back into the soil.

Soil. This is where the roots of the grass plants grow.

COOL-, TRANSITIONAL, AND WARM-SEASON TURF AREAS

◁ Identify which zone you're in so that you select the right grass type for your weather.

Turf Types

Turf types are divided into three main categories: warm season, cool season, and transitional. *Warm season* turf grasses actively grow during the summer and are dormant (and brown) during the winter. These grasses grow best in the southern third of the United States. *Transitional* area turf types will grow moderately well all year, and can handle extreme temperature swings while actively growing. Lawns in those areas are usually a blend of several types of grass. *Cool season* grasses are actively growing during the fall and spring and often go dormant and turn brown during hot, dry summer months. They will go dormant during the coldest winter months, but usually stay green.

To have a lush lawn, you must select a turf type that grows well in your area. All grasses listed on page 220 can be managed organically. St. Augustine grass is probably the most difficult to manage this way, and requires the most inputs. Stay away from it when possible.

Most cool-season lawns are a blend of several different grass types, while most warm season lawns are a single grass type. Cool-season grasses tend to have a more uniform look across grass types, while warm-season grasses have widely variable textures and leaf widths.

Lawn Care the Organic Way

Good care goes a long way toward eliminating lawn problems. It also helps to adjust your expectations of what a healthy lawn should look like. For an organic gardener, a weed or two here and there does not signify the end of the world. My motto is, "If it's green, it's good."

MOWING

Regardless of the turf type, the higher you mow, the better off the plants will be. Long grass blades equal deep root systems, and deeper root systems help plants cope with drought. The ideal mowing height depends on the type of grass but a good rule of thumb to maintain healthy grass plants is to never remove more than one-third of the plant at one time. If heavy rains have caused you to be off the lawn for an extended period, you might have to mow twice, separated by a few days, in order to bring the grass back to the desired height. When possible, mow on the taller end of the range.

Mowing heights. Average mowing heights for popular turf grasses will vary with the cultivar, so always research the exact height for your lawn grass. Here are some standard recommendations:

- Bahia: 2 to 3 inches
- Bermuda: 1 to 2 inches
- Bluegrass: 3 to 4 inches
- Bluestem: 4 to 5 inches
- Buffalograss: 4 to 5 inches
- Carpetgrass: 2 to 3 inches
- Centipede: 2 to 3 inches
- Chewings fescue: 2 to 3 inches

- Hard fescue: 3 to 4 inches
- Perennial rye: 3 to 4 inches
- Red fescue: 3 to 4 inches
- Seashore paspalum: 1 inch
- St. Augustine: 2 to 4 inches
- Tall fescue: 3 to 4 inches
- Zoysia: 2 to 3 inches

ADDITIONAL MOWING TIPS

- **Mulch the grass clippings and leave them on the lawn.** Contrary to popular belief, using a mulching mower does not cause problems with thatch. Grass clippings add valuable nitrogen to the soil to feed microbes and plant roots.

- **Don't scalp the grass.** There is a misguided notion that at the end of the growing season you should mow the grass down to almost bare earth. Because the growing tip of a grass plant is near the ground, doing this can kill the grass completely.

△ Use a mulching mower to naturally return nutrients to the lawn.

△ Water deeply and infrequently to encourage deep root growth.

- **Mow in the late afternoon.** At this time of day the dew has dried, which lessens the chance of disease spread. The grass will also not be stressed by a hot, baking sun.

- **Sharpen blades in the spring.** Mowing with sharp blades results in a cleaner cut and a neater looking lawn.

Watering

In an ideal world, you'd never have to water the lawn. Unfortunately, even in areas where rain is mostly a sure thing, droughts happen and sometimes you have to water in order to keep the lawn alive. Note that I did not say "green." Watering grass enough to keep it alive doesn't always green it up, nor should that be the goal. During hot, dry summers, cool season grasses will often go dormant and turn brown. Watering once a week (as long as water restrictions aren't in place) is usually enough to keep it alive.

If you do water the lawn, follow these tips:

- **Water in the early morning.** This will allow grass to dry off before nighttime, preventing the spread of diseases.

- **Water deeply and infrequently.** It is better to water once a week but give the lawn a thorough soaking than it is to water shallowly every day. Like mowing high, deep watering promotes deep root growth.

- **Water when the grass needs it, not on a set schedule.** If you're getting regular rain, don't waste clean water on turf. You can tell the grass needs water when it takes on a grayish sheen. It also will not spring back up quickly when you walk on it. Sometimes the leaf blades will curl up—the plant's way to reduce surface area to lose water.

- **Take environmental conditions into account.** The amount of sunlight your lawn receives will impact watering frequency. More sun equals more frequent watering. The type of soil you have will impact how much water to apply each time. Coarse, well-drained soil equals less volume required to saturate the soil.

Dethatching

All lawns have thatch. The question is, does your lawn have a thatch *problem*? A buildup of thatch usually happens when the lawn grass grows faster than what soil organisms are equipped to process in terms of dead stems and other organic matter. Overfertilizing and lack of a healthy soil microbial ecosystem are the main culprits behind thatch buildup. Grasses growing on acidic soils tend to have more thatch problems than grasses growing on neutral soils because the bacteria that thrive on grass residue also thrive in alkaline conditions. Acidic soil conditions will select for a limited microbial community and, as a result, thatch builds up quicker. Pesticides that interfere with soil biology can also cause a buildup in thatch.

A thin thatch layer of ¼ inch or so provides some insulating qualities against soil moisture fluctuation but thicker thatch can cause problems. A thick thatch layer can end up being a haven for pests and diseases and it can prevent water from soaking into the lawn efficiently. Lastly, when thatch gets too thick, grass plants will start growing their roots into the thatch rather than the soil, which makes the plants more susceptible to fluctuations in moisture.

If the grass feels extra spongy when you walk on it or it doesn't seem to perk up after watering, you might have a thatch problem. Cut out a small 2- to 3-inch square of turf, and look at the layer between the soil and the green grass leaves. If it's taller than ½ inch, dethatch and also test your soil pH to determine whether you need to lime the lawn.

HOW TO DETHATCH

You can get a thatch rake to manually remove the thatch layer, but this is a lot of work. If you have a large yard, it's impractical. It's better to rent a dethatcher. This piece of power equipment will lift the thatch layer from the soil, at which point you can rake the thatch out and compost it.

Usually, dethatching is followed by aerating and a compost or humus application, which is another step in adding organic matter to the soil, improving soil structure, and thus promoting the conditions for a healthy lawn.

The best time to dethatch is when the weather is mild and the grass is actively growing. Late spring and early summer are the best times to dethatch warm season lawns. Early fall is the best time to dethatch in cool season areas. Lawns in transitional areas can be done in late spring or early fall. The key is to dethatch after grasses are actively growing, but to also allow at least a few weeks of sustained growth after thatching before peak summer heat or cold winter frost sets in.

△ Dethatch when necessary to reduce pest and disease problems.

△ Core aerating reduces problems with compaction and literally opens up an opportunity to amend the soil in the lawn.

Aerating

Lawns grow best when the soil is healthy, and part of keeping it healthy is maintaining good structure. Compacted soils have slow percolation rates and low oxygen-holding capacity, all of which puts the plants growing in them at risk. Thatch buildup that prevents water penetration can cause structural problems that lead to compaction. Excessive foot traffic from recreational activities can also cause compaction. Heavy soils can naturally become compacted over time due to regular maintenance activities such as mowing.

Part of growing an organic lawn is relying on organic inputs to fertilize, and the best way to fertilize is by adding compost. You can't just dump three inches of compost on top of the lawn and walk away, though. You also can't really "dig" it into the lawn the way you would a vegetable garden bed. You can top-dress the lawn annually with a thin layer of compost without aerating first, but aerating will make the process go faster by opening up holes into which you can rake the compost. That puts the compost exactly where earthworms and other soil organisms can work on incorporating it into the soil. Fertilizing is not the main reason to aerate, though. The primary reason to aerate is to maintain good soil structure to facilitate good plant health.

To determine whether your lawn needs to be aerated, try to push a tined fork into the soil when the soil is slightly moist. If you cannot, it is likely the soil is compacted. Aerate at the same time you would dethatch—when the grass is actively growing.

HOW TO AERATE

You can rent core-aerating machines at home improvement centers, though they are heavy and somewhat difficult to operate. It's easier to just pay a lawn company to do the aerating for you and you can then spread the compost yourself. Beware of aerators that simply punch holes into the soil—pushing soil down rather than

△ Take soil samples from several areas of the lawn to get an accurate report regarding necessary soil amendments.

Trees and Shrubs

Back Lawn

Flower Bed

Front Lawn

△ Mow with a mulching mower and leave clippings on the lawn to add nutrients back into the soil.

lifting cores out. That can cause more problems with compaction rather than alleviating them.

Mow and then water the lawn two or three days before aerating. The soil should be moist but not wet. Run the aerator across the entire lawn in both directions to ensure even coverage. After aerating, rake a thin layer (¼- to ½-inch) of fine compost over the lawn and water it. This will mix compost with the aerated soil cores, and get much of the mixture back into the aeration holes. Any material remaining on the surface will break down and reincorporate into the topsoil horizon. It's fine for the surface material to go back into the holes made by aerating.

Fertilizing

It would be nice if you could forego fertilizer altogether, but that's not an option for lawns. Grasses are hungry plants and in order for them to stay healthy and out-compete the weeds, they require food. Using a mulching mower to chop up grass clippings and shred leaves into tiny pieces is one way to get organic matter back into the soil. The other way is to fertilize.

Before applying any fertilizer, check the soil pH. If the pH is too low, add lime according to soil test and lime package instructions. If the pH is too high, add aluminum sulfate according to soil test and package instructions. When the pH is off, plants won't be able to access nutrients contained in any type of fertilizer.

Fertilizer and pH requirements differ depending on grass type. Some need more nitrogen than others. All grass types benefit from a light application of compost once or twice per year. If you're going to aerate, top-dress with compost after aerating. Otherwise, plan to spread a ½-inch layer of screened compost across the lawn in the late spring and early fall.

When growing turf that requires higher nitrogen levels, look for fish emulsion, kelp meal, alfalfa meal, and other high-nitrogen organic products to provide mid-season feedings. I like to use a balanced fertilizer with low amounts of phosphorus, such as an 8-2-4 or all-purpose turf fertilizer. Many states have banned phosphorus from turf grass fertilizers. Your local garden center should stock an organic lawn fertilizer or two that is appropriate and legal for your state. Follow the label when applying lawn fertilizer, so you know how frequently to apply, and to ensure that you put the right amount down and are not wasting it or polluting things down-stream.

Do not fertilize warm season grasses with high-nitrogen fertilizers during the fall and winter, as the grass is dormant. And do not fertilize cool season grasses with high nitrogen fertilizers in late spring or early summer for the same reason.

When lawn remediation techniques are necessary, always wait until the lawn is actively growing. This ensures the lawn can recover quickly after a treatment.

Fall Cleanup and Winter Maintenance

Top on the cultural care list for healthy organic lawns is fall cleanup. Leaves should always be either mowed and mulched, or raked and composted. Do not leave large mats of leaves sitting on the lawn. That's a one-way ticket to fungal problems.

In warm areas, mow the lawn to the lowest recommended height until it goes dormant, at which point you can clean and put away the mower. In cool areas, mow at a lower height and continue to mow as long as the grass is growing. Avoid mowing when the soil is saturated and do not scalp the lawn!

Organic Lawn Care Troubleshooting

The sooner you wrap your brain around the idea that a few weeds or weed patches in the lawn is normal, the happier you'll be with your organic lawn maintenance program. Many "problems" with the lawn are more like minor annoyances. Unless the problems result in a full-scale death of the turf, many are not even worth worrying about. Many can be avoided or solved with good cultural care or manual intervention, rather than with chemicals.

Here are some of the most common lawn problems and the organic solutions. If you find yourself with a problem that isn't on this list, consult with your local cooperative extension agency or local garden center for solutions. Contractors may seem like the logical go-to, but many turf care contractors are intent on profit, not solutions that are crafted especially for your situation. If you trust your contractor, then by all means, ask them for an action plan.

WEEDS

Good care will get you 90 percent of the way in terms of weed management. Mowing grass at the tallest recommended height will cause the grass plants to shade out any weed seeds that might germinate. It will also encourage deep roots that out compete weeds.

There is some indication that corn gluten meal can be used as a pre-emergent herbicide to prevent annual weed seeds from sprouting. It should be applied in early spring and again in the late summer to prevent winter weeds. Research has shown it takes at least 4 to 5 years of application to get consistent weed suppression. When using this in your garden spaces, remember that it inhibits *all* seeds from germinating in the soil. While this is great to keep weeds down, it also means desirable species will also be kept from germinating.

Otherwise, your best method of control beyond good cultural care is to hand-dig or pull large weeds and continually mow smaller weeds before they have the chance to set seed. Prevention is key. By pulling weeds *before* they go to seed, you'll eliminate a lot of headaches. You can burn weeds with a propane-powered, hand-held flame-thrower or spray individual plants with vinegar, but it's just as easy to pull them. If trying the vinegar route, use horticultural vinegar—it's much stronger than household vinegar. Just know that the acidity in vinegar will lower the localized pH around the weeds you're spraying.

BROWN PATCHES

Brown spots, both regular and irregular, are usually a symptom of bacterial or fungal diseases. Staying off the grass when it is wet is one way to control the spread of these diseases. Keep the thatch layer under control, avoid overfertilizing, and promote good airflow to prevent fungal diseases.

Should you have to treat a fungal problem with a fungicide, make sure to top-dress with worm castings to reinoculate the soil with good bacteria and fungi. Just like when you get sick and have to take antibiotics—to speed recovery you have to follow the antibiotics with a course of probiotics to reinoculate yourself with good bacteria.

DOG SPOTS

Isolated patches caused by pet urine require repair, if not prevention. Thoroughly flush out the affected area with water. Then spread a thin layer of compost or worm

△ Weedy lawns are often the result of poor soil.

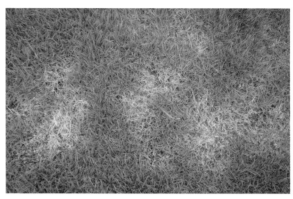

△ Brown patches can be caused by bacterial or fungal problems.

△ Fairy ring fungus.

△ Controlling grubs will help control problems with moles and Japanese beetles.

castings on top and overseed to reestablish the grass. Then take your dog for a walk next door or at the dog park!

MUSHROOMS

"Fairy ring" is a common lawn affliction characterized by a ring of mushrooms sprouting in the yard, or a ring of turf that is greener than the surrounding turf. These are just the evidence of fungi growing underground, feasting on decomposing organic matter and releasing nitrogen. Eventually the fungi will consume the food source and wear itself out. If you find them annoying, you can rake and remove them from your lawn.

INSECT PROBLEMS

Chinch bugs, mole crickets, and sod webworms are three common lawn insect pests. Most can be prevented with good cultural controls, such as keeping the thatch layer to a minimum, watering appropriately and avoiding drought stress,

△ Voles eat plant roots, and their "tunnels" are usually on the surface of the soil.

△ Moles eat grubs and tunnel under the surface of the soil.

and mowing at the proper height. There are organic remedies available for all three as well, including insecticidal soap for chinch bugs, Neem oil for mole crickets, and *Bt* and pyrethrin for sod webworms. As always, any sort of chemical intervention should be a last resort, as all chemical remedies will disrupt the natural balance and ecosystem of the lawn.

GRUBS

Grubs are the larvae of different types of beetles. They eat plant roots and attract moles. Grub damage is most pronounced during August and September and is characterized by widespread dead patches in an irregular pattern across the lawn. You can easily peel up pieces of lawn where grubs are present.

You can control the grubs of Japanese beetles by applying milky spore in the fall when the larvae are active in the soil. Other grub species can be controlled with healthy populations of soil-dwelling nematodes. Enhance beneficial nematode populations by adding compost and/or worm castings. Beneficial nematodes can also be purchased and applied to the lawn if the soil isn't hosting a sufficient population to control grubs.

MAMMALS

Moles and voles are some of the worst mammal problems in lawns. Moles tunnel underground looking for grubs, so if you treat the grubs, the mole problem will go away as well. Mole tunnels are raised mounds with live grass above them, while vole tunnels tend to be pathways of destruction through the grass. Voles eat plant roots, so they are the more destructive mammalian pest. Unfortunately, they are also protected in many states. If you have a mole or vole problem, one solution might be to get a cat or a terrier dog.

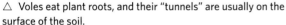

⬅ Moss grows in shady, sandy, highly acidic soils.

PROLIFERATION OF MOSS

Moss will only out-compete grass and take over in areas if conditions are not favorable for grass to grow. Moss thrives in shady areas with compacted soil that has low fertility and an abnormally high or low pH. Before you decide to try to treat moss, ask yourself, "Is it really important to have a lawn here?" If you just want something green and easy care, leave the moss. Some people even plant moss "lawns" because they're easy to grow and have a Zen-like feel.

Growing a No-Mow Lawn

Lawn replacement is a hot topic, especially in areas with water-conservation pressure. If you don't need actual turf grass for family activities or homeowner association requirements, consider replacing some or all of your turf grass with low-growing native ornamental grasses, perennials, or groundcovers.

Gardeners living in cool season areas can plant the "No Mow Lawn Seed Mix" from Prairie Nursery, or the "Eco lawn" from Wildflower Farm, which are blends of different fescue grasses designed to grow with a single annual mowing. These are great eco-friendly options for all you homeowners living in within the confines of a homeowner association.

Gardeners living in warmer areas can get the lawn look by planting dwarf mondo grass and other groundcovers in large swaths. Sedges make good low-traffic lawn plants in areas with plenty of rainfall. Thyme, sedum, oregano, and other drought-tolerant groundcovers will do the job in drier climates.

△ Eco-Lawn is a good option for organic gardeners in cool-season turf areas.

12

Reduce, Reuse, Repurpose, Recycle: The Organic Lifestyle

We close our discussion of practical organic gardening with a reminder of the Golden Rule as it applies to organic gardeners: leave the earth better than when you found it, and leave it as you would have others leave it. The forest is a perfect example of the Golden Rule in action. It replenishes everything it needs with two inputs—sun and rain.

Organic gardening as presented in this book is a lifestyle choice that pays it forward and builds its merit in cascading form. A single organic backyard garden can combine with others to form a community of gardens. Many communities join to form a region. Regions join together to form states, states to countries, countries to continents, continents to the entire planet!

◁ Organic gardening is all about recycling.

△ Use old hoses to soften sharp edges.

△ Always drill drainage holes in the bottom of repurposed containers.

Organic Gardening Extends Beyond the Soil

"Use it up, wear it out, make it do, or live without" was the mantra of the Great Depression, and it still holds true today. Being organic in the garden goes beyond just our choices for soil, fertilizer, and pest control. Organic also means we do well with what we have on hand rather than following the consumer mentality of always acquiring more. Have a hose that pops a hole? Fix it. When you wear out that hose completely, use it to edge a bed to remind you where the garden bed begins so you don't run over emerging plants in spring. Or carefully cut it apart lengthwise and use it to soften the edge of a sharp container, such as the edge of a 50-gallon drum that you cut in half and are repurposing as a planter. A moment of consideration can probably find a use in the garden for just about any used item. Even if your garden aesthetic would never lead you to use an old hose like this, I encourage you to continue considering alternate garden uses for everyday items that wear out their original purpose.

Incorporating Repurposed Elements into Your Garden

Gardeners have one of the greatest hobbies. We get to create beauty and cultivate joy in our gardens, our backyards, our landscapes, and our homes. What better way to incorporate your own particular aesthetic than by using repurposed items in the garden? Items from your home can be repurposed outside when they have lost their original purpose inside. If a dish or bowl gets a crack, it may not hold soup anymore, but it sure can hold potting soil! Recycling unique containers or design elements in your garden is sustainable, and fits into the big picture to reduce our impact on the planet.

Repurposing Vintage Finds

Some of my favorite garden containers are ones I found while going about my everyday life. Garage sales, side of the road scores, and in some cases, vintage shops have the greatest discoveries. I almost picked up an old non-functioning piano once but it was a little too big for just me to handle! I love using old dressers as planting benches. You can place potted plants on top, and open the drawers up to fill with soil and plants. Finding treasures to reuse in a new way helps reduce the amount of new containers you have to buy, which in turn reduces your impact on the planet.

Recycling Soil from Containers into the Garden

In addition to recycling and repurposing containers, tools, and other items in the garden, potting soils should always be recycled into the garden. There are a number of ways to do this—and some ways not to do it.

- **Recycling in place.** As long as the plants remained healthy all season, just remove all plant material (stems, leaves, and roots), fluff up the soil, and add any additional potting soil necessary to bring the soil level back up to the top of the container. Don't forget to add new fertilizer at planting time. This reuse can happen a number of times until the potting soil is the consistency of flour. Once it reaches this stage, it's time to recycle the potting soil into garden beds as a soil amendment.

- **Keep potting soil out of the compost pile.** Never add potting soil into your compost pile. Placing large amounts of potting soil into your compost can cool off the pile and keep it from cooking down. Mixing potting soil into the veggie garden is a better choice if it has broken down into small particles. Plus, it adds organic matter to the beds.

- **Dealing with diseased potting soil.** If potting soil has been contaminated by a diseased plant, I dump it out in a specific area in the back of a bed where it can break down slowly over time. Don't blend it into the soil, as this could contaminate your beds with the same plant disease. Just leave it alone and let nature take its course. Alternately, you can put it out for the municipal composting program when you place other materials out for collection. Bag it along with other items in the approved brown paper bags. Large-scale municipal composting programs can get the pile size and temperatures needed to break down small amounts of spent and diseased potting soil.

Recycling Trees

If you celebrate Christmas, I hope you recycle your tree. You can leave it at the edge of your property to help build habitat for birds and insects, or drop it off at a community recycling program that turns used Christmas trees into wood chips to beautify local community landscapes.

Fallen trees can be a headache, but why not turn lemons into lemonade? Large tree trunks can be milled into boards for a table. Large branches can be used to create unique design features, start a fence line, create an arbor, or border new raised beds. In many cases the natural look can exceed the aesthetics of the typical milled boards from a hardware store. Short segments of trunk can become garden benches or pedestals for holding pots. Some branches may be suitable for plugging with mushroom spores to grow an edible crop.

The Final Word: Reduce Consumption

At the heart of organic philosophy is a devoted effort to use everything you have on hand and at home before heading out to buy more. You can propagate your own plants. You can collect your own seeds to sow the following year. You can divide plants to increase the size of your garden. You can trade with friends, sharing the wealth and dishing out plants. This gives each gardener new plants to enjoy, all without spending a penny on new things. Plus, you'll get to practice a new skill— propagation!

Growing your own herbs and veggies is also part of the movement to reduce consumption at the store. It saves you money and it's incredibly satisfying to eat the fruits of your garden labor. Herbs are a perennial way to reduce grocery store consumption while saving landfills and recycling bins from all that plastic packaging. Plus, if you grow your own herbs, they will be fresh and available 365 days a year when you need them. Having parsley or rosemary growing outside on Thanksgiving Day when you realize you've forgotten it at the store? Priceless!

Whether reducing, reusing, repurposing, or recycling, by skipping buying something new, you help to reduce overall consumption and lessen your impact on the planet. Part of the organic paradigm is to do no harm on the planet on which we all live so the Earth can sustain us for as long as possible.

May your organic gardening bring you satisfaction, and may it bring the planet improved health.

Mark Highland
The Organic Mechanic

Resources

ATTRA Sustainable Agriculture Program
National Center for Appropriate Technology (NCAT)
program provides information and technical assistance
on all aspects of sustainable agriculture
1-800-346-9140
www.attra.ncat.org

Bugwood Image Databse system
Searchable database of insect images for insect ID
www.images.bugwood.org

Cornell University
School of Integrative Plant Science—
Horticulture Resources
www.hort.cals.cornell.edu

**Food and Agriculture Organization of the
United Nations**
Food security, biodiversity, ecosystem services, and
soils reference information
www.fao.org/about/en

National Sustainable Agriculture Coalition
Alliance of grassroots organizations advocating for
federal policy reform to advance sustainable agriculture
goals
www.sustainableagriculture.net

Organic Consumers Association
Organization campaigning for health, justice,
and sustainability
www.organicconsumers.org/organlink

Organic Farming Research Institute
Resources for organic and transitioning farmers
831-426-6606
www.ofrf.org/policy/resources

Sustainable Agriculture Research & Education
Grants and education to advance innovations in
sustainable agriculture
www.sare.org

Texas A&M University
AgriLife Organic Vegetable Gardening
www.aggie-horticulture.tamu.edu/organic/crops/
vegetable-gardening

The Rodale Institute
Research and advocacy for organic farming methods
610-683-1400
www.rodaleinstitute.org

The University of California–Santa Cruz
Center for Agroecology and Sustainable Food Systems
casfs.ucsc.edu/about/publications

The University of Florida
Organic Gardening Resources
www.edis.ifas.ufl.edu/topic_organic_gardening

The University of Wisconsin–Madison
UW Organic and Sustainable Agriculture
Research Extension
www.uworganic.wisc.edu

**USDA Natural Resource Conservation
Service (NRCS)**
Soils, vegetation, and environment reference
information
www.nrcs.usda.gov/wps/portal/nrcs/site/national/home

Acknowedgments

One is the loneliest number. How anyone could attempt to write a book alone is a sad thought indeed. I cannot begin to thank all those who had a hand in helping me learn the cumulative knowledge base I have today. But, of course, I will try.

Certainly, my grandparents get a lot of credit for gardening with me as a child, stirring my love of this rock we call Earth. My parents get many thanks for raising a boy who loves to play in the dirt.

Whether it was at the University of Florida with Dr. David Clark, Dr. James Barrett, and Dr. Bijan Dehgan, or at the University of Delaware with Dr. Jeffry Fuhrmann, Dr. James Swasey, Dr. Elaine Ingham, and Dr. Casey Sclar—my thanks to all of you who pushed me to explore science and discover new horizons in horticulture and agriculture.

From the barefoot days in the research fields at UF to the greenhouses of Oregon, friends have been an integral part of this journey. Farming friends Tucker Taylor, Michael McMahan, Chi-wei Chu, and Hiro Myoshi taught me many secrets of successful organic farming.

Once I moved back east, the staff of Longwood Gardens imparted much knowledge, and for that I am eternally thankful. People are always the greatest asset of any organization. The team at Longwood and the greater horticulture community in the Delaware Valley were no exception to this rule. To my Longwood Fellows, thanks for pushing me forward. Many, many thanks to all who taught me a lesson or two on organic gardening in Pennsylvania, including Dale Hendricks, Jeff Lynch, Suzanne Wainwright-Evans, Andrew Bunting, Dan Benarcik, Peggy Anne Montgomery, Lloyd and Candy Traven, Tim Mountz, and Claire Murray.

Thank you to Katie Elzer-Peters for being my "book whisperer" friend and for all the advice and knowledge—you were epically awesome to work with! To Shawna Coronado for organic inspiration and believing in me. To the Longwood crew (you know who you are!) and my water buddies for all your encouragement and support. To the Mogreena Garden Project for garden camaraderie and your dedication to feeding peoples' bodies and spirits. To everyone who helped start Organic Mechanics, especially those company members who believed in my vision of starting an earth-friendly potting soil company. To all my gardening friends who have taught me lessons or traded plants with me, thank you all for contributing to the soundtrack of my life. May all your gardens flourish and your plants multiply!

Image Credits

Bill Kersey: 23 (top), 26, 31 (bottom), 37, 41, 75, 89, 101, 102, 128, 218, 219, 224 (right)

Brie Arthur: 19 (all), 148 (top left), 189 (bottom)

Bryan Trandem: 103 (bottom)

Costa Farms: 202 (top right)

Crystal Liepa: 27, 32 (top), 36 (both), 47, 49, 54 (both), 65, 77 (both), 78, 83, 84 (top), 85 (bottom), 91 (both), 92 (all), 93 (all), 96, 103 (top), 115 (right), 118, 124, 143 (left), 157 (right), 199, 206 (left), 221 (left), 229 (top)

Dale Hendricks: 180 (bottom)

Daniel Smith: 198

DieterO/Wikimedia Commons: 148 (bottom right)

EcoLawn: 229 (bottom)

Frank Fox/Wikimedia Commons: 29 (bottom)

iStock: front and back cover, 1, 3, 5, 7, 21, 39, 51, 87, 109, 127, 153, 177, 201, 215, 223, 231

Jessica Walliser: 97, 107, 200, 204 (top right), 206 (right), 208, 210, 232 (right)

Katie Elzer-Peters: 12 (both), 15, 16, 46 (both), 48 (top), 69 (top left and right), 90, 99 (top), 105, 112 (both), 115 (left), 117 (left), 129 (left), 141 (right), 150, 178 (top), 179 (bottom), 180 (top right), 191, 197 (top left and right, bottom left), 202 (top left), 204 (top left), 207 (left and bottom right)

Mark Highland: 9, 10, 24 (all), 32 (bottom left and right), 67 (left), 71, 72, 73 (all), 74 (all), 76, 80, 155 (all), 156, 157 (left), 162 (all), 163, 164, 167 (all), 169 (all), 170 (all), 171, 174 (all), 175 (both), 183 (all), 204 (bottom left and right), 232 (left)

Michael Swan: 50

Pam Powell: 197 (bottom right)

Roger Griffith/Wikimedia Commons: 148 (top right)

Ryan Somma/Wikimedia Commons: 189 (top)

Scott Nelson/Flickr: 117 (right)

Shunwen Lu: 31 (top)

Shutterstock: 13, 17 (all), 20, 22 (all), 23 (bottom), 29 (top and middle), 30 (top), 38, 42, 43, 44, 45, 48 (bottom), 52, 53, 58 (top), 60 (both), 62, 66 (both), 67 (right), 69 (bottom left and right), 70, 82 (both), 84 (bottom), 85 (top), 86, 99 (bottom), 108, 126, 129 (right), 130, 132 (both), 133, 134 (both), 138, 139 (all), 141 (left), 142 (both), 143 (right), 144 (all), 148 (middle left and right, bottom left), 152, 154, 159, 168, 176, 178 (bottom left and right), 179 (top), 180 (top left), 184, 185 (bottom left and right), 186, 187 (both), 188 (all), 190, 192, 193 (all), 194, 195, 196, 202 (bottom), 205 (both), 207 (top right), 214, 217 (both), 221 (right), 224 (left), 227 (all), 228 (both), 230

Sonya Harris: 185 (top)

Troy Marden: 6, 56, 61

William Wergin/Richard Sayre/Wikimedia Commons: 30

Index

To my wife and children, who sacrificed the most to allow me to write this book.
Amy, may the sun always rise and set on our garden. Lucius and Flinn,
may you live an organic life of love and prosperity. To my family, you were the soil,
sunshine, and water that made me grow. Thank you for this life!

About the Author

Photo by Chris Starr

It was on a beautiful piece of Illinois farmland that Mark Highland pushed his first shovel into garden soil. Once he "grew up," Mark achieved a B.S. in Environmental Horticulture from the University of Florida, then moved to Oregon to help start a USDA Certified Organic farm and run a design-build landscape company. Mark then moved back east to focus his M.S. degree studies in the Longwood Graduate Program on compost and potting soil. After the Longwood Graduate Program, Mark started The Organic Mechanic Soil Company, LLC in 2006. Mark has served as a board member for the Ecological Landscape Alliance (ELA), as a consultant for the Environmental Protection Agency (EPA) and Institute for Local Self-Reliance (ILSR), and has received the Young Professional Award from the Perennial Plant Association (PPA). Mark currently resides in Chester County, PA, with his wife, Amy, and their two children.